THE WAR: A MEMOIR

MARGUERITE DURAS

THE WAR

A MEMOIR

TRANSLATED FROM THE FRENCH
BY BARBARA BRAY

PANTHEON BOOKS, NEW YORK

First American Edition

Translation Copyright © 1986 by Barbara Bray

Duras, Marguerite.
The war.

Translation of: La douleur.
1. Duras, Marguerite—Biography.   2. Authors,
French—20th century—Biography.   3. World War,
1939-1945—Personal narratives, French.   I. Title.
PQ2607.U8245Z46413   1986   843'.912 [B]   85-43435
ISBN 0-394-55236-9

Book Design by Gina Davis

MANUFACTURED IN THE UNITED STATES OF AMERICA

FOR NICOLAS RÉGNIER
AND FRÉDÉRIC ANTELME

I

THE WAR

I found this diary in a couple of exercise books in the blue cupboards at Neauphle-le-Château.

I have no recollection of having written it.

I know I did, I know it was I who wrote it. I recognize my own handwriting and the details of the story. I can see the place, the Gare d'Orsay, and the various comings and goings. But I can't see myself writing the diary. When would I have done so, in what year, at what times of day, in what house? I can't remember.

One thing is certain: it is inconceivable to me that I could have written it while I was actually awaiting Robert L.'s return.

How could I have written this thing I still can't put a name to, and that appalls me when I reread it? And how could I have left it lying for years in a house in the country that's regularly flooded in winter?

The first time I thought about it was when the magazine Sorcières asked me for a text I'd written when I was young.

The War is one of the most important things in my life. It can't really be called "writing." I found myself looking at pages regularly filled with small, calm, extraordinarily even handwriting. I found myself confronted with a tremendous chaos of thought and feeling that I couldn't bring myself to tamper with, and beside which literature was something of which I felt ashamed.

April

Opposite the fireplace and beside me, the telephone. To the right, the sitting-room door and the passage. At the end of the passage, the front door. He might come straight here and ring at the front door. "Who's there?" "Me." Or he might phone from a transit center as soon as he got here. "I'm back—I'm at the Lutetia to go through the formalities." There wouldn't be any warning. He'd phone. He'd arrive. Such things are possible. He's coming back, anyway. He's not a special case. There's no particular reason why he shouldn't come back. There's no reason why he should. But it's possible. He'd ring. "Who's there?" "Me." Lots of other things like this do happen. In the end they broke through at Avranches and in the end the Germans withdrew. In the end I survived till the end of the war. I must be careful; it wouldn't be so very extraordinary if he did come back—it would be normal. I must be careful not to turn it into something extraordinary. The extraordinary is unexpected. I must be sensible: I'm waiting for Robert L., expecting him, and he's coming back.

The phone rings. "Hello? Any news?" I must remind myself the phone's used for that sort of thing, too. I mustn't hang up, I must answer. Mustn't yell at them to leave me alone. "No, no news." "Nothing? Not a sign?" "Nothing." "You know Belsen's been liberated? Yes, yesterday afternoon . . ." "I know." Silence. Am I going to ask again? Yes. "What do you think?" I ask. "I'm beginning to get worried." Silence. "You mustn't get disheartened, you must hold on, you're not the only one, alas—I know a mother with four children . . ." "I know, I'm sorry, I have to go out, goodbye." I put the phone down. I haven't moved from where I was. It's wrong to move too much, a waste of energy, you have to save all your strength to suffer.

She said, "You know Belsen's been liberated?" I didn't know. One more camp liberated. She said, "Yesterday afternoon." She didn't say so, but I know the lists of names will arrive tomorrow morning. I must go down and buy a paper and read the list. No. I can hear a throbbing in my temples getting louder and louder. No, I won't read the list. For one thing, I've been trying the lists for three weeks, and that's not the way. The more lists there are, the fewer names they'll have on them. There'll be lists right up to the end, but he'll never be on them while I read them. It's time to move. Get up, take a few steps, go to the window. The medical school is still there. And the people going by—they'll still be walking past when I hear he's never coming back. A notification of death. They've started sending them out recently. A ring at the door. "Who is it?" "A social worker from the town hall." The throbbing in my head is still there. I must stop it. His death is in me, beating in my head. No mistake about it. I must stop the throbbing, stop my heart, calm it down—I must help it, it will never calm down on its own. I must stop my reason from flying off at a tangent, out of my head. I put my coat on and go downstairs. The concierge is there. "Good day, Madame L." She doesn't seem any different from usual. Nor does the street. Outside it's April.

In the street I am like a sleepwalker. My hands are thrust deep into my pockets, my legs move forward. I must avoid the newsstands. Avoid the transit centers. The Allies are advancing on all fronts. A few days ago that mattered. Now it doesn't matter at all. I've stopped reading the communiqués. There's no point—now they'll advance all the way. Light, the light of day, flooding in on the mystery of Nazism. April, it will happen in April. The Allied armies are surging over Germany. Berlin is burning. The Red Army continues its victorious advance in the south, they're past Dresden. They're advancing on all fronts. Germany is driven back within its own borders. The Rhine has been crossed, everyone knew it would be. Remagen, that was the great day of the war. It was after Remagen that it started. In a ditch, face down, legs drawn up, arms outstretched, he's dying. Dead. Beyond the skeletons of Buchenwald, his. It's hot all over Europe. The advancing Allied armies march past him. He's been dead for three weeks. Yes, that's what's happened. I'm certain of it. I walk faster. His mouth is half open. It's evening. He thought of me before he died. The pain is so great it can't breathe, it gasps for air. Pain needs room. There are far too many people in the streets; I wish I were on a great plain all alone. Just before he died he must have spoken my name. All along the roads of Germany there are men lying like him. Thousands, tens of thousands, and him. He who is at once one of the thousands of others and, just for me, completely separate and distinct from the thousands of others. I know all one can know when one knows nothing. At first they evacuated them, then at the last minute they killed them. War is a generality, so are the inevitabilities of war, including death. He died speaking my name. What other name could he have spoken? Those who live on generalities have nothing in common with me. No one has anything in common with me. The street. At this moment there are people in Paris who are laughing, especially the young. I have nothing left but enemies. It's evening, I must go home and wait by the phone. Over there it's evening, too. It's getting darker in the ditch, his mouth is in darkness now. A slow red sun over Paris. Six years of war ending. The great event of the century. Nazi Germany is crushed. So is he, in the ditch. Everything is at an end. I can't stop walking. I'm thin, spare as stone. Beside the ditch is the parapet of the Pont des Arts, the Seine. To be exact, it's to the right of the ditch. They're separated by the dark. Nothing in the world belongs to me now except that corpse in a ditch. It's a red evening. The end of the world. My death's not directed against anyone. Just a simple death. I shall merely have died. It's a matter of indifference to me, the moment when I die is a matter of indifference to me. When I die I won't rejoin him, I'll just stop waiting for him. I'll tell D., "It's best to die—what use would I be to you?" I'll be clever and die for D. while I'm still alive, then when I actually die it'll be a relief to him. I make this base calculation. I must go home.

D.'s waiting for me. "Any news?" "No." People don't say hello or how are you to me any more. They say, "Any news?" And I say, "No." I go and sit by the phone, on the divan. I don't speak. D.'s uneasy. When he's not looking at me he looks worried. He's been lying for a week. I say, "Say something." He's stopped saying I'm crazy, that I have no right to drive everyone else mad too. Now he scarcely even says, "There's no reason why he shouldn't come back like anyone else." He smiles. He's thin too, his whole face creases when he smiles. I don't think I could hold out without D. there. He comes every day, sometimes twice a day. He stays. He switches on the light in the sitting room, he's been here an hour already, it must be nine o'clock, we haven't had dinner yet.

D. is sitting at a distance from me. I stare at a point outside the black window. D. looks at me. Then I look at him. He smiles at me, but it isn't genuine. Last week he still came close to me, held my hand, said, "Robert will come back, I swear it." Now I know he wonders if it wouldn't be better to stop keeping my hopes up. Sometimes I say, "I'm sorry." After an hour I say, "How is it we haven't had any news?" He says, "There are still thousands of deportees in the camps the Allies haven't reached—how could they let you know?" That goes on for a long while, until I ask D. to swear Robert will come back. Then D. swears Robert L. will come back from the concentration camps.

I go into the kitchen and put the potatoes on. I stay there, lean my forehead on the edge of the table, shut my eyes. D., back in the apartment, doesn't make a sound, there's only the hum of the gas. It might be the middle of the night. Suddenly it bursts in on me, the obvious: he's been dead for a fortnight. Fourteen days, fourteen nights, abandoned in a ditch. The soles of his feet exposed. With the rain, the sun, the dust of the victorious armies all falling on him. His hands are open. Each hand dearer than my life. Known to me. Known like that to me alone. I cry out. Slow footsteps in the sitting room. D. comes in. I feel two strong, gentle hands around my shoulders, raising my head from the table. I'm pressed against D. I say, "It's awful." "I know," says D. "No, you can't know." "I do know," says D., "but try, we can do anything if we try." I'm at the end of my tether. It's a comfort to have someone's arms around you. Sometimes you might almost think you feel better. For a minute you can breathe. We sit down to eat. But at once I want to throw up again. The bread is bread he hasn't eaten, the bread for lack of which he died. I want D. to go. I need room again to suffer. D. goes. The apartment creaks under my step as I move. I turn out the lights, go into my room. I go slowly so as to gain time, so as not to stir up the things in my head. If I'm not careful I won't sleep. And when I don't get any sleep, the next day is much worse. I fall asleep beside him every night, in the black ditch, beside him as he lies dead.

April
I go to the center at the Gare d'Orsay. I have a lot of trouble getting them to admit the Tracing Service of

Libres,* the paper I founded in September 1944. They said our service wasn't official. The BCRA† is already installed and doesn't want to surrender its place to anyone else. To begin with I set myself up there by stealth, with forged papers and permits. We managed to collect a lot of information, which was published in *Libres,* about movements of prisoners and transfers from one camp to another. Also a good many personal messages. "Tell such-and-such a family their son is still alive—I saw him yesterday." They threw me and my four colleagues out. Their argument was, "Everyone wants to be here, but that's impossible. Only Stalag secretariats will be allowed." I object that our paper is read by seventy-five thousand relatives of prisoners and deportees. "Very sorry, but the rules don't allow any unofficial services here." I say our paper's different, it's the only one that brings out special issues with lists of names. "That's not a good enough reason." This is a senior official in the repatriation service of the Frenay ministry.‡ He looks very preoccupied, and is worried and distant. But polite. He says, "I'm sorry." I say, "I'll fight it out." I set off in the direction of the offices. "Where are you going?" "I'm going to do my best to stay." I try to slip in among a line of prisoners of war

* *Libres:* Plural form of the adjective *libre,* meaning "free." N.B.: Footnotes throughout this edition are by the translator.

† BCRA: The Bureau Central de Renseignement et d'Action (Central Office for Intelligence and Action) had been set up by the Free French in London to coordinate intelligence, including that supplied by the Resistance networks in France.

‡ Henri Frenay, one of the great leaders of the Resistance in France (head of the *Combat* group), was made head of the Ministry for Prisoners, Deportees, and Refugees in the autumn of 1944.

that fills the whole width of the corridor. The official points at them and says, "As you like, but be careful—they haven't been through quarantine yet. Anyhow, if you're still here this evening I'm afraid I'll have to turn you out." We found a little pine table that we put at the entrance to the circuit the men have to follow. We question the prisoners. Many of them come over to speak to us. We collect hundreds of bits of information. I work without looking up, I don't think of anything but spelling the names right. Every so often an officer, easily recognizable among the others, in a tight khaki shirt and throwing his chest out, comes up and asks us who we are. "Tracing Service? What's that? Have you got a pass?" I show a false one. It works. Then there's a woman from the repatriation service. "What do you want with these men?" I explain that we're asking them for news. She asks, "And what do you do with it?" She's a young woman with platinum blond hair, in a navy blue suit with shoes to match, sheer stockings, and red nails. I say we print it in a paper called *Libres*, for prisoners and deportees. She says, "*Libres*? So you're not ministry?" No. "Have you got permission to do this?" She's becoming rather chilly. I say, "We're taking permission." Things are made easier for us by the extreme slowness of the prisoners' progress. From the time they get off the train it takes them two-and-a-half hours to reach the first stage of the circuit, the identity check. It'll take even longer for the deportees, because they haven't any papers and they're infinitely wearier, most of them ready to drop. An officer comes back, forty-five years old, tightly buttoned uniform, very curt. "What's all this?" We explain again. He says, "We've already got a tracing service." I venture to ask, "How do you get the news to the families? We know it'll be a good three months before all of them will have been able to write." He looks at me and bursts out laughing. "You don't understand. It's not a question of news. We're collecting information about Nazi atrocities." He goes away, then comes back. "How do you know they're telling you the truth? What you're doing is very dangerous. You do know members of the Milice* hide among them, don't you?" I don't say it's a matter of indifference to me if members of the Milice don't get arrested. I don't say anything. He goes away. Half an hour later a general comes straight up to our table, accompanied by a noncommissioned officer and the young woman in the navy blue suit, who is also an NCO. "Your papers," he says, like a cop. I show them. "Not good enough. You're allowed to work standing up, but I don't want to see this table here any more." I object that it doesn't take up much room. He says, "The minister has expressly forbidden anyone to set up a table in the main hall." He calls two scouts, who take the table away. We'll work standing up. From time to time the radio comes on, a program that alternates swing with patriotic tunes. The line of prisoners gets longer. Every so often I go to the ticket counter on the far side of the hall. "Still no deportees?" "No." Uniforms all over the station. Women in uniform, repatriation services. We wonder where these people have sprung from, and these clothes, impeccable after six years of occupa-

* The Milice Française (French Militia), founded on January 30, 1943, was a collaborationist political and paramilitary police force, made up of volunteers and first headed by Laval.

tion, these leather shoes, these hands, this tone of voice, scathing and always scornful whether it expresses anger, condescension, or affability. D. says, "Take a good look at them. Don't forget." I ask where all this has come from, why it's suddenly here among us, and above all who it is. D. says, "The Right. That's what it's like. What you see here is the Gaullist staff taking up its positions. The Right found a niche in Gaullism even in the war. You'll see—they'll be against any resistance movement that isn't directly Gaullist. They'll occupy France. They think they constitute thinking France, the France of authority. They're going to plague the country for a long while, we'll have to get used to dealing with them." The women refer to the prisoners as "the poor boys." They talk to one another as if they were in a drawing room: "My *dear* . . ." Almost all speak with the accent of the French aristocracy. They're here to inform the prisoners about train timetables. They wear the special smile of women who want people to see both how tired they are and what efforts they're making to conceal it. It's stifling in here. They're really very busy. Every so often some officers come to see them, they exchange English cigarettes. "Indefatigable as ever?" "As you see, Captain!" They laugh. The hall echoes with footsteps, whispered conversations, tears, groans. People keep on arriving. Truck after truck. From Le Bourget. The prisoners are dumped at the center in groups of fifty. Whenever a group arrives the music strikes up: "*C'est la route qui va, qui va, qui va, et qui n'en finit pas . . .*"* For larger groups it's the "Marseillaise." There are silences be-

* "It's a road that goes on and on and never ends."

tween the songs, but very short ones. The "poor boys" look at the hall, they all smile. They're surrounded by repatriation officers. "Come along, boys, get in line!" They get in line and go on smiling. The first ones to arrive at the identity window say, "Slow work!" but still smile pleasantly. When they're asked for information they stop smiling and try to remember. These last few days I was at the Gare de l'Est, where one of the women rebuked a soldier from the Legion and pointed to her stripes. "No salute, my boy? Can't you see I'm a captain?" The soldier looked at her. She was young and pretty. He laughed. The woman hurried off, saying, "What manners!" I go to see the head of the center to sort out the matter of the Tracing Service. He gives us permission to stay, but at the end of the circuit by the office where baggage is checked. I stick it out as long as there are no convoys of deportees. Some of them are arriving at the Lutetia, but for the moment there's only the odd one now and then at Orsay. I'm afraid of seeing Robert L. suddenly appear. It's arranged with my companions that as soon as any deportees are announced I leave the center and only come back when they've gone. When I do come back the others make signs to me as I approach. "Nothing. None of them knows Robert L." In the evening I take the lists to the paper. Every evening I tell D., "I won't go back to Orsay tomorrow."

April 20
Today's the day when the first batch of political deportees arrives from Weimar. They phone me from the

center in the morning. They say I can come, the deportees won't be there till the afternoon. I go for the morning. I'll stay all day. I don't know where to go to bear myself.

Orsay. Outside the center, wives of prisoners of war congeal in a solid mass. White barriers separate them from the prisoners. "Do you have any news of so-and-so?" they shout. Every so often the soldiers stop; one or two answer. Some women are there at seven o'clock in the morning. Some stay till three in the morning and then come back again at seven. But there are some who stay right through the night, between three and seven. They're not allowed into the center. Lots of people who are not waiting for anyone come to the Gare d'Orsay, too, just to see the show, the arrival of the prisoners of war and how the women wait for them, and all the rest, to see what it's like; perhaps it will never happen again. You can tell the spectators from the others because they don't shout out, and they stand some way away from the crowds of women so as to see both the arrival of the prisoners and the way the women greet them. The prisoners arrive in an orderly manner. At night they come in big American trucks from which they emerge into the light. The women shriek and clap their hands. The prisoners stop, dazzled and taken aback. During the day the women shout as soon as they see the trucks turning off the Solferino Bridge. At night they shout when they slow down just before the center. They shout the names of German towns: "Noyeswarda?"* "Kassel?" Or Stalag numbers:

* The author's note at this point reads: "I haven't been able to find this name in the atlas. I've probably spelled it as it sounded to me."

"VII A?" "III A Kommando?" The prisoners seem astonished. They've come straight from Le Bourget airport and Germany. Sometimes they answer, usually they don't quite understand what's expected of them, they smile, they turn and look at the Frenchwomen, the first they've seen since they got back.

I can't work properly; of all the names I record none is ever his. Every five minutes I want to give it up, lay down the pencil, stop asking for news, leave the center for the rest of my life. At about two in the afternoon I go to ask what time the convoy from Weimar arrives. I leave the circuit and look for someone to ask. In a corner of the main hall I see about ten women sitting on the floor and being addressed by a colonel. I go over. The colonel is a tall woman in a navy blue suit with the cross of Lorraine in the lapel. Her white hair has been curled with tongs and blue-rinsed. The women look at her. They look harassed, but listen open-mouthed to what she says. The floor around them is littered with bundles and cases tied with string. A small child is sleeping on one of the bundles. The women are very dirty and their faces look tired and shocked. Two of them have enormous bellies. Another woman officer stands nearby, watching. I go over and ask her what's going on. She looks at me, lowers her eyes, and says delicately, "STO volunteers."* The colonel tells them to get up and follow her. They rise and follow her. The reason they look so frightened is that

* STO: The Service du Travail Obligatoire (Forced Labor Service), introduced in February 1943, was an organized deportation of French workers. Some people actually volunteered to work in Germany.

they've just been booed by the wives of the prisoners of war waiting outside the center. A few days ago I saw some other STO volunteers arrive. Men, this time. Like the other men they were smiling when they arrived, but gradually they realized and then their faces too looked shocked. The colonel points to the women and asks the young woman in uniform who's just told me who they are, "What are we supposed to do with them?" The other one says, "I don't know." The colonel must have told them they were scum. Some of them are crying. The pregnant ones stare into space. The colonel has told them to sit down again. They sit down. Most of them are factory workers, their hands blackened by the oil of German machinery. Two of them are probably prostitutes, their faces are made up and their hair dyed, but they must also have worked with machinery, they've got the same grimy hands as the others. A repatriation officer comes up. "What's all this?" "STO volunteers." The colonel's voice is shrill, she turns toward the volunteers and threatens, "Sit down and keep quiet . . . Do you hear? Don't think you're just going to be let go . . ." She shakes her fist at them. The repatriation officer goes over to the bunch of volunteers, looks at them, and there, right in front of them, asks the colonel, "Do you have any orders?" The colonel: "No, do you?" "Someone mentioned six months' detention." The colonel nods her beautiful curly head: "Serves them right . . ." The officer blows puffs of smoke—Camels—over the bunch of volunteers, who've been following the conversation with eyes wild with apprehension. "Right!" he says, and goes off, young, elegant, a born horseman, his Camel in his hand. The volunteers watch, looking for some indication of the fate awaiting them. There is none. I stop the colonel as she makes off. "Do you know when the convoy from Weimar arrives?" She gives me a searching look. "Three o'clock," she says. She goes on looking at me, weighing me up, and says with just a touch of irritation, "No point in cluttering up the place waiting. It'll only be generals and prefects. Go home." I wasn't expecting this. I think I insult her. I say, "What about the others?" She bridles. "I can't stand that kind of attitude! Go and complain somewhere else, my dear." She's so indignant she goes and tells a small group of other women in uniform, who listen, are also indignant, and look at me. I go up to one of them and say, "Isn't *she* waiting for anyone?" The woman looks at me, scandalized, and tries to calm me down. She says, "The poor thing's got so much to do, her nerves are in shreds." I go back to the Tracing Service at the end of the circuit. Soon afterward I go back to the main hall. D.'s waiting for me there with a forged pass.

About three o'clock there's a rumor: "They're here." I leave the circuit and station myself at the entrance to a little passage opposite the main hall. I wait. I know Robert L. won't be there. D. is beside me. His job is to go and question the deportees to find out if they know Robert L. He's pale. He doesn't pay any attention to me. There's a great commotion in the main hall. The women in uniform fuss around the volunteers and make them sit on the floor in a corner. The main hall is empty. There's a pause in the arrivals of prisoners of war. Repatriation officers go back and forth. The loudspeaker has stopped too. I hear people saying, "The minister," and see Frenay among the officers. I'm still standing at the entrance to the little corridor. I watch the entrance. I know Robert L. can't possibly be there. But perhaps D. will manage to find out something. I don't feel well. I'm trembling, cold. I lean against the wall. Suddenly, there's a hum of voices: "Here they are!" Outside, the women haven't shouted. They haven't applauded. Suddenly, two scouts emerge from the passage carrying a man. He has his arms around their necks. They've joined hands to support his legs. He's in civilian clothes, shaven, he appears to be in great pain. He's a strange color. He must be crying. You couldn't say he's thin, it's something else—there's so little of him left you wonder if he's really alive. But no, he is alive, his face is convulsed by a terrifying grimace. He doesn't look at anything. Not at the minister, not at the hall, not at the flags—nothing. The grimace may be a laugh. He's the first deportee from Weimar to arrive at the center. Without realizing it I've moved forward, I'm in the middle of the hall with my back to the loudspeaker. Two more scouts come in carrying another, an old man. Then another ten or eleven arrive. These appear to be in better condition, they can walk, with help. They're installed on garden benches that have been set out in the hall. The minister goes over to them. The second one to arrive, the old man, is weeping. You can't tell if he's as old as all that, he may be only twenty, you can't tell his age. The minister comes over, takes off his hat, goes up to the old man, holds out his hand. The old man takes it, but doesn't know it's the minister's.

A woman in a blue uniform bawls at him: "It's the minister! He's come to meet you!" The old man goes on crying, he hasn't even looked up. Suddenly I see D. sitting down beside him. I'm very cold, my teeth are chattering. Someone comes up to me: "Don't stay here, there's no point, it's making you ill." I know him, he's a fellow from the center. I stay. D. has started to talk to the old man. I go over it all quickly in my head. There's one chance in ten thousand the old man might have met Robert L. In Paris they're beginning to say the army has lists of survivors from Buchenwald. Apart from the old man crying and the rheumatics, the others don't seem in too bad condition. The minister's sitting with them, as are the senior officers. D. talks to the old man at length. I don't look at anything but D.'s face. I feel this is taking a very long time. I move very slowly toward the bench, into D.'s field of vision. He notices, looks at me, and shakes his head to signify, "No, he doesn't know him." I move away. I'm very tired, I feel like lying down on the ground. Now the women in uniform are bringing the deportees mess tins. They eat, and as they eat they answer questions. What's so remarkable is that they don't seem interested in what's said to them. I'll find out next day from the papers that among these people, these old men, are General Challe; his son Hubert Challe, who had been a cadet at Saint-Cyr and who was to die that night, the night of his arrival; General Audibert; Ferrière, head of the state tobacco industry; Julien Cain, director of the Bibliothèque Nationale; General Heurteaux; Marcel Paul; Professor Suard of the faculty of medicine at Angers;

Professor Richet; Claude Bourdet; the brother of Teitgen, the minister of information; Maurice Nègre; and others.

I leave the center at about five in the afternoon and go home along the river. The weather's fine, it's a lovely sunny day. I can't wait to get back, to shut myself up with the telephone, be back again in the black ditch. As soon as I leave the embankment and turn into the rue du Bac, the city is far away again and the Orsay center vanishes. Perhaps he will come back after all. I don't know any more. I'm very tired. I'm very dirty. I've been spending part of the night at the center, too. I must make up my mind to take a bath when I get in, it must be a week since I stopped washing. I feel the cold so badly in the spring, the idea of washing makes me shudder, I have a sort of permanent fever that doesn't seem to want to go away. This evening I think about myself. I've never met a woman more cowardly than I am. I go over in my mind other women who are waiting like me—no, none is as cowardly as that. I know some who are very brave. Extraordinary. My cowardice is such that it can't be described, except by D. My colleagues in the Tracing Service think I'm crazy. D. says, "No one has the right to destroy himself like that, ever." He often tells me, "You're sick. You're a madwoman. Look at yourself—you look like nothing on earth." I can't understand what people are trying to say to me. [Even now, transcribing these things from my youth, I can't understand the meaning of those expressions.] Not for a second do I see the need to be brave. Perhaps being brave is my form of cowardice.

Suzy is brave for her little boy. The child we had, Robert L. and I, was born dead, he died in the war too: doctors didn't usually go out at night during the war, they hadn't enough gas. So I'm on my own. Why should I husband my strength? There's nothing for me to fight for. No one can know my struggle against visions of the black ditch. Sometimes the vision gets the upper hand and I cry out or leave the house and walk the streets of Paris. D. says, "When you think about it later on you'll be ashamed." People are out in the streets as usual, there are lines outside the shops; there are some cherries already, that's what the women are waiting for. I buy a paper. The Russians are in Strausberg, perhaps even farther, on the outskirts of Berlin. The women standing in line for cherries are waiting for the fall of Berlin. I'm waiting for it too. "Then they'll see, then they'll find out what's what," people say. The whole world is waiting for it. All the governments in the world are agreed. When the heart of Germany stops beating, say the papers, it will be all over. Zhukov has a ring of guns only a hundred yards apart pounding the city from a range of less than forty miles. Berlin is in flames. It will be burned right down to the roots. German blood will flow among its ruins. Sometimes you think you can smell the blood. See it. A prisoner who's a priest brought a German orphan back to the center. He held him by the hand, was proud of him, showed him off, explained how he'd found him and that it wasn't the poor child's fault. The women looked askance at him. He was arrogating to himself the right to forgive, to absolve, already. He wasn't returning from any suffering, any waiting. He was taking the liberty of exercising the right to forgive and absolve there and then, right away, without any knowledge of the hatred that filled everyone, a hatred terrible yet pleasant, consoling, like a belief in God. So what was he talking about? Never has a priest seemed so incongruous. The women looked away, they spat upon the beaming smile of mercy and light. They ignored the child. A total split, with on the one side the solid, uncompromising front of the women, and on the other just the one man, who was right, but in a language the women didn't understand.

April

Monty's supposed to have crossed the Elbe, but it's not certain, Monty's aims are not so clear as Patton's. Patton is forging ahead. He's reached Nuremberg. Monty is said to have reached Hamburg. David Rousset's wife phones: "They've reached Hamburg. They won't say anything about the camps at Hamburg-Neuengamme for several days." She's been very worried the last few days, and with reason. David was there, in Bergen-Belsen. The Germans were shooting people. The Allied advance is very swift. The Germans haven't time to move people, so they're shooting them. We don't yet know that sometimes, when they don't have time to shoot them, they leave them where they are. Halle has been wiped out. Chemnitz has been taken and left far behind in a drive on Dresden. Patch is mopping up in Nuremberg. Georges Bidault is talking to President Truman about the San Francisco conference. I walk the streets. We are tired, tired. In *Libération-Soir*: "Vaihingen will never be heard of again. On the maps, the pale green of the forests will stretch right down to the Enz. . . . The watchmaker was killed at Stalingrad, the barber served in Paris, the village idiot occupied Athens. Now the main street is desperately empty, its cobblestones turned belly up, like dead fish." A hundred and forty thousand prisoners of war have been repatriated. So far no figure for deportees. Despite the efforts of the ministry services, it's all been too much. The prisoners wait for hours in the Tuileries gardens. It is announced that this year's film festival will be exceptionally brilliant. Six hundred thousand Jews were arrested in France. It's already said that one in a hundred will come back; that's six thousand. We still believe it—that he might come back with the Jews. It's a month since he might have sent us news. So why shouldn't he come with the Jews? It seems to me I've waited long enough. We're tired. There's to be another arrival of deportees from Buchenwald. There's a baker's shop open, maybe I should buy some bread, so as not to waste the coupons. It's criminal to waste coupons. There are some people who are not waiting for anything. There are some who've stopped waiting. The evening before last, on the way back from the center, I went to give a message to a family in the rue Bonaparte. I rang the bell, someone answered, I said, "I'm from the Orsay center. Your son's coming back. He's well." The woman knew already, the son had written five days ago. D. was waiting for me. I said, "They knew about their son already, he'd written. So they *can* write." D. didn't answer. That was two days ago. Every day I wait less. In the evening my concierge waylays me as I go in. She asks me to go and see Madame Bordes, the concierge at the school. I say I'll go in the morning, that there's nothing for Madame Bordes to worry about because today it was Stalag VII A that came back, no question yet of III A. The concierge runs to tell her. I slowly climb the stairs; I'm breathless with fatigue. I've stopped going to see Madame Bordes, but I'll try to go in the morning. I'm cold. I go and sit down again on the divan by the telephone. It's the end of the war. I don't know if I feel sleepy or not. For some time now I haven't known what sleep is. I wake up, so I know I've been asleep. I get up and lean my forehead against the windowpane. Down below is the Saint-Benoît restaurant, full up, a hive of activity. They've got a secret menu for those who can pay. It's not normal to wait like this. I'll never know anything. All I know is that he was hungry for months and didn't see another scrap of bread until he died, not even once. The condemned man's last wishes—his weren't granted. Since April 7 I've had a choice. He might have been among the two thousand who were shot at Belsen. At Mittel-Glattbach they found fifteen hundred bodies in a charnel house. Everywhere, on all the roads, there are huge columns of wild-looking men being taken they don't know where, the *kapos* don't know either, nor do the officers. Today the twenty thousand survivors of Buchenwald salute the fifty-one thousand dead. Shot the day before the Allies arrived. Think of being killed just a few hours before. Why? People say, "So they wouldn't tell." In some camps the Allies have found bodies still warm. What do you do at the last moment when you're losing the war? You break the china, you throw stones and smash windows, you kill dogs. I don't bear a grudge against the Germans any more, you can't call it that any more. For a while I could bear a grudge against them, it was quite plain and clear, I wanted to massacre all of them, the whole population of Germany, wipe them off the face of the earth, make it impossible for it to happen again. But now I can't tell the difference between the love I have for him and the hatred I bear them. It's a single image with two faces: on one is him, his breast exposed to the German, the hope of twelve months drowning in his eyes. On the other side are the eyes of the German who's aiming at him. Those are the two faces of the image. I have to choose between the two, him rolling over into the ditch or the German slinging his submachine gun over his shoulder and walking away. I don't know if I should be taking him in my arms and letting the German get away, or forgetting Robert L. and grabbing the German who killed him and gouging out the eyes that didn't see his. For three weeks I've been thinking they must be stopped from killing when they run away. But no one's come up with anything. They could have sent teams of parachutists to hold the camps for the twenty-four hours until the Allies arrived. Jacques Auvray had been trying to arrange it since August 1944. But it hadn't been possible because Frenay didn't want the credit to go to a resistance movement. He was minister for prisoners of war and deportees, but he couldn't do it himself. So he let the Germans shoot them. Now they'll go on shooting them until the last concentration camp is liberated. Nothing can be done to stop them now. Sometimes, in my double image, Frenay stands behind the German, looking on. It's nice standing with my forehead against the cold glass. I can't hold my head up any more. My legs and arms are heavy, but not so heavy as my head. It's not a head any more, it's an abscess. The glass is cool. D. will be here in an hour. I shut my eyes. If he comes back we'll go to the seaside, that's what he'd like best. I think I shall die anyway. Even if he comes back. If he rang at the door: "Who is it?" "It's me, Robert L."—all I'd be able to do is open the door and die. If he comes back we'll go to the seaside. It'll be summer, high summer. Between the time when I open the door and the time when we find ourselves by the sea, I am dead. In a kind of posthumous existence I see that the sea is green and that there's an orange-colored beach, sand. Inside my head, a salt breeze that prevents thought. I don't know where he is while I see the sea, but I know he's alive. That he's there, somewhere on the earth, breathing. So I can lie down on the beach and rest. When he comes back we'll go to the sea, a warm sea. That's what he'll like best, and what will do him most good. He'll arrive, he'll go to the beach, he'll stand there looking at the sea. It'll be enough for me to look at him. I don't ask anything for myself. Head against the window. It may well be me who's weeping. Out of six hundred thousand, one who's weeping. The man looking at the sea is him. In Germany the nights were cold. There on the beach, he goes out in his shirt-sleeves and he talks to D. They're deep in conversation. I'll be dead. As soon as he comes back I shall die, it can't be otherwise, it's my secret. D. doesn't know. I've chosen to wait for Robert like this, unto death. That's my business. I go back to the divan and lie down. D. rings at the door. I go and answer. "Nothing?" "Nothing." He comes in and sits down by the divan. I say, "I don't think there's much hope left." D. looks exasperated and doesn't answer. I go on, "Tomorrow's the twenty-second of April and twenty percent of the camps have been freed. I saw Sorel at the center, and he said one in fifty would come back." D. hasn't the strength to answer but I go on. The doorbell rings. It's Robert L.'s brother-in-law. "Well?" "Nothing." He nods, thinks for a moment, then says, "It's a question of communications. They can't write." They say, "There's no longer any regular mail in Germany." I say, "Maybe, but there *has* been news of those who were in Buchenwald." I remind them that the convoy of August 17, the one Robert L. was in, is known to have arrived at Buchenwald. "But how do you know he wasn't transferred somewhere else at the beginning of this year?" I tell them to go away, to go home. For a while I hear them go on talking, then less and less. There are long pauses in the conversation, and then suddenly the voices are back again. I feel someone take me by the shoulder—it's D. I'd fallen asleep. D. shouts, "What's the matter with you, going to sleep like that?" I go to sleep again. When I wake up, M. has gone. D. goes and gets a thermometer. I have a temperature.

In my feverish state I see her again. She'd stood in line for three days with the others in the rue des Saussaies, outside the Ministry of the Interior. She must have been about twenty. She had an enormous belly jutting out. She was there because of one of those who were shot: her husband. She had been notified to come and collect his things. She was shivering in spite of the heat.

She talked and talked, she couldn't stop. She was collecting his things because she wanted to see them again. Yes, the baby was due in two weeks, it would never know its father. She read out his last letter over and over again to her neighbors in the line. "Tell our child I was brave." She talked, she wept, she couldn't keep anything in. I think of her because she isn't waiting any more. I wonder if I'd recognize her if I met her on the street. I've forgotten her face, all I can remember about her is that enormous belly jutting out and how she held out the letter as if she wanted to give it away. Twenty years old. They offered her a camp stool. She tried to sit down, but stood up again. She could only bear herself standing up.

Sunday, April 22, 1945
D. has slept here. By last night they still hadn't phoned. I must go and see Madame Bordes. I make myself some strong coffee and take a corydrane tablet. The giddiness will go, and the nausea. I'll feel better. It's Sunday, so there's no mail. I take D. a cup of coffee. He looks at me and smiles very sweetly. "Thank you, Marguerite dear." I shout, "No!" I can't bear to hear my name. After a dose of corydrane you perspire heavily and your temperature drops. Today I don't go either to the center or to the printer's. I must buy a paper. Another photograph of Belsen, a long pit with rows of corpses in it, bodies thinner than anyone has ever seen before. "The front is less than three miles from the heart of Berlin." "The Russian communiqué abandons its usual reserve." Monsieur Pleven pretends to govern

France, he announces an overhaul of wages and higher farm prices. Mr. Churchill says, "We haven't long to wait now." Perhaps the Allies and the Russians will join up today. Debrû-Bridel protests against the forthcoming elections, to be held without the deportees and prisoners of war. On page two of *FN** it says a thousand deportees were burned alive in a barn near Magdeburg on the morning of April 13. In *Art and War* Frédéric Noël says, "Some people think war brings artistic revolution, but war really operates on other levels." Simpson takes twenty thousand prisoners. Monty has had a meeting with Eisenhower. Berlin is burning: "From Stalin's command post he must be able to see a strange and terrible sight." There have been twenty-seven air raid alerts in Berlin in the last twenty-four hours. There are still some people alive there. I arrive at Madame Bordes's place. The son is in the lobby. The daughter is weeping on a divan. The lodge is dark, dirty, and untidy. Full of Madame Bordes's tears; like France. "A fine how do you do," says the son. "She won't get up any more." Madame Bordes is in bed. She looks at me, disfigured with crying. She says, "So that's that." I repeat, "There's no reason to be so upset, Stalag III A isn't back yet." She thumps on the bed with her fist and shouts, "That's what you told me a week ago!" "I'm not making it up—read the paper!" You can't tell from the papers!" She's obstinate and won't look at me. She says, "You say none of them are back, but the streets are full of them." They know I often go to Frenay's ministry and the Tracing Service. If I

* *FN*: Organ of the *Front National*, a largely Communist resistance organization.

handle her right Madame Bordes will get up again for another few days. Such weariness. It's true III A must have been liberated two days ago. Madame Bordes waits for me to speak. Out there on the roads a man drops out of the column. A hail of bullets. I feel like leaving her to die. But the young son is looking at me. So I read out the lists of those "due back," and I use my imagination. I go and buy some bread and go back upstairs to the apartment. D. is playing the piano. He's always played the piano whatever happened. I sit down on the divan. I don't like to tell him not to play. It hurts my head and makes me feel like throwing up. But it *is* strange just the same, being left so completely without news. They've got other things to do. Millions of men are awaiting the final consummation. Germany has been beaten to a pulp. Berlin is in flames. A thousand cities have been razed to the ground. Millions of civilians are fleeing; Hitler's electorate has been routed. Fifty bombers take off every minute. Here they're busy with local elections. And with repatriating prisoners of war. There's been talk of commandeering civilian cars and apartments, but they haven't dared do it for fear of offending their owners. De Gaulle's against it. De Gaulle has always put his North African Front before his political deportees. On April 3 he uttered these criminal words: "The days of weeping are over. The days of glory have returned." We shall never forgive. He also said: "Among all the places on earth where fate has chosen to issue its decrees, Paris has always been a symbol . . . It was so when the surrender of Paris confirmed the triumph of Prussian Germany in January 1871 . . . It was so in the famous days of 1914 . . . It was so again in 1940." He doesn't mention the Commune. He says the defeat of 1871 confirmed the existence of Prussian Germany. For de Gaulle, the Commune confirms the depraved tendency of the people to believe in their own existence, their own strength. De Gaulle, by definition lauder of the Right—whenever he speaks he addresses himself to it and it alone—would like to bleed the people of their vital strength. He'd like them to be weak and devout, he'd like them to be Gaullist, like the bourgeoisie, he'd like them to *be* bourgeois. De Gaulle doesn't talk about the concentration camps, it's blatant the way he doesn't talk about them, the way he's clearly reluctant to credit the people's suffering with a share in the victory for fear of lessening his own role and the influence that derives from it. It's he who insists on having the local elections now. He's a regular officer. After three months the people I know judge him and reject him forever. The women hate him, too. Later on he'll say: "The dictatorship of the sovereign people entails risks that must be alleviated by the responsibility of one man." Has he ever mentioned the tremendous danger involved in the responsibility of leadership? The Reverend Father Panice, speaking about the meaning of revolution in Notre-Dame, said: "Popular uprising, general strike, barricades, and so on. It would make a good film. But does it make anything more than a semblance of revolution? Does it mean real, fundamental, lasting change? Look at 1789, 1830, 1848. After a period of violence and a few political upheavals, the people tire, they have to earn their living and start work again." The people must be discouraged. The Reverend Father also said:

"When it comes to order, the Church has no hesitation, it is in favor." De Gaulle has declared a day of national mourning for the death of Roosevelt. No national mourning for the dead deportees. We have to keep on the right side of America. France is going into mourning for Roosevelt. For the people, mourning will not be worn.

You don't exist any more in comparison with his waiting. More images pass through your head than there are on all the roads in Germany. Bursts of machine gun fire every minute inside your head. And yet you're still there, the bullets aren't fatal. Shot in transit. Dead with an empty stomach. His hunger wheels around in your head like a vulture. You can't give him anything. You can always hold out a piece of bread in the void. You don't even know if he still has need of bread. You buy honey, sugar, pasta. You say to yourself, If he's dead I'll burn the lot. Nothing can help the way his hunger burns you. People die of cancer, of car accidents, but no, they don't die of hunger, they're finished off first. What hunger has wrought is completed by a bullet in the heart. I'd like to give him my life. I can't even give him a bit of bread. You can't call this thinking, everything's in a state of suspended animation. Madame Bordes and I exist only in the present. We can think in terms of one more day to live. We can't think in terms of three more days. For us, to buy butter or bread for three days hence would be an insult to God's discretion. We cling to God, cleave to something like God. "You'll have uttered every possible stupidity," says D.," every possible kind of nonsense." So will Madame

Bordes. There are people now who say, "We must think through what's happening." D. tells me, "You should try to read. One ought to be able to read whatever happens." You've tried to read, you'll have tried everything, but the words don't connect with one another any more, though you suspect the connection does exist. But sometimes you think it doesn't, that it never has, that the truth is the here and now. Another connection obsesses us: the one linking their bodies to our lives. Perhaps he's already been dead for two weeks, lying peacefully in the black ditch. Already vermin are crawling over him, swarming inside him. A bullet in the back of the neck? In the heart? Between the eyes? His pale lips against the German earth, and me still waiting because it's not quite certain, perhaps it'll take another second. Because it may be that he'll die from one second to the next, but that it hasn't happened yet. So second by second our life ebbs away too, every possibility vanishes; or equally well, life returns to us, every possibility revives. Perhaps he's in a column on the march, perhaps he's moving along one step at a time, head bowed, perhaps he won't take the next step, he's so tired. Perhaps he wasn't able to take that next step two weeks ago? Six months? An hour? A second? There's no room in me for the first line of any book that is already written. No book is up-to-date for Madame Bordes and me. We're in the vanguard of a nameless battle, a battle without arms or bloodshed or glory; we're in the vanguard of waiting. Behind us stretch the ashes of civilization and of all the thought amassed through the ages. Madame Bordes won't listen to any theories. In her head, as in mine, the only happenings are upheavals without substance, lapses and collapses of we know not what, distances seeming to open toward a way out, then disappearing, shrinking almost unto death; there's nothing but suffering everywhere, bleeding and cries. That's why thought can't function. It's not part of the chaos, it's constantly being supplanted by it, helpless against it.

April—Sunday

Still on the divan near the phone. Today, yes, today Berlin *will* be taken. They announce it every day, but today really will be the end. The papers tell us how we'll know: by the sirens going off for the last time. The last time in the war. I don't go to the center any more, I won't go back there again. Some arrive at the Lutetia, some at the Gare de l'Est. Or the Gare du Nord. It's all over. Not only will I not go back to the center, I won't move at all. So I think, but I thought that yesterday, too, and at ten in the evening I took the metro and went and rang D.'s doorbell. He opened the door. Took me in his arms. "Nothing new all of a sudden?" "No. I'm at the end of my tether." Then I went away again. I wouldn't even go in, I only wanted to see D., to check that he hadn't got some special sign on his face, some lie about death.

There in my apartment, suddenly, on the stroke of ten, fear had entered in. Fear of everything. And I'd found myself outside in the street.

All of a sudden I had looked up and the apartment had changed. So had the light from the lamp, it was suddenly yellow. And suddenly certainty, certainty burst in: he's dead. Dead. Dead. The twenty-first of April, died on the twenty-first of April. I'd stood up and gone to the middle of the room. It had happened in the space of a second. No more throbbing in my head. Not now. My face falls apart, changes. I fall apart, come undone, change. There's no one in the room where I am. I can't feel my heart any more. Horror mounts in a slow flood, I'm drowning. I'm so afraid, I'm not waiting any more. Is it all over? Is it? Where are you? How can I tell? I don't know where he is. I don't know where I am either. I don't know where we are. What's this place called? What sort of place is it? What is all this business? What's it all about? Robert L., who is he? No more pain. I'm on the point of realizing there's no longer anything in common between this man and me. I might just as well be waiting for another. I no longer exist. So, if I no longer exist, why wait for Robert L.? If she wants to wait, why not wait for another? She and this man no longer have anything in common. Who is this Robert L.? Has he ever existed? What is it that makes him Robert L.? Why should he be waited for, he rather than another? What is she really waiting for? What other waiting? What has she been playing at for the last couple of weeks, working herself up with this waiting? What's going on in that room? Who is she? D. knows who she is. Where is D.? She knows she can see him and ask him for explanations. I must see him because something new has happened.

I went to see him. Apparently nothing had happened.

Tuesday, April 24

The phone rings. I wake up in the dark. I turn on the light, see the alarm clock: half-past five. Still night. I hear someone say, "Hello? . . . what?" It's D., who's been sleeping in the next room. I hear, "What? What's that you say? Yes, this is Robert L.'s place . . ." Silence. I'm standing by D., who's holding the phone. I try to grab it. The conversation goes on. D. won't let go. "What news?" Silence. Someone's talking from the other side of Paris. I try to snatch the phone, it's too much, unbearable. "So? Friends, you say?" D. puts the phone down and says, "Some friends of Robert's are at the Gaumont." She shrieks, "No! I can't believe it!" D. has picked up the phone again: "And what about Robert?" She tries to grab it again. D. doesn't say anything, he just listens, the phone is his. "And that's all you know?" He turns to her. "They last saw him two days ago. He was alive." She doesn't try to grab the phone again. She's on the floor, fallen on the floor. Something gave way at the words saying he was alive two days ago. She offers no resistance. It bursts out through her mouth, her nose, her eyes. It has to come out. D. has put down the phone. He speaks her name, "Marguerite, Marguerite dear." He doesn't come over, doesn't lift her up, he knows she's untouchable. She's occupied. Leave her alone. It comes out everywhere as water. Alive. Alive. Someone says, "Marguerite, Marguerite dear." Two days ago, as alive as you or me. It comes out as moans, too, cries. It comes out however it likes. Comes out. She offers no resistance. D. says, "We must go there, they're at the Gaumont, waiting for us, but let's make ourselves some coffee before we go."

He said that so that she would have some coffee. He laughs. He can't stop talking. "What a guy! . . . How could we ever have imagined they'd . . . He knows a thing or two . . . Probably hid at the last minute . . . And we thought he couldn't take care of himself because of his manner." D.'s in the bathroom. He said, "Because of his manner." She's leaning against the kitchen cupboard. It's true that he seems different from most people. He was absent-minded. He looked as if he never noticed anything, he was always off in the heart of absolute goodness. She still leans against the kitchen cupboard. Always off in the heart of the absolute pain of thought. She makes the coffee. D. repeats, "We'll have him here in a couple of days." The coffee's ready. The taste of hot coffee. He's alive. I dress very quickly. I've taken a corydrane tablet. I've still got a temperature, I'm bathed in sweat. The streets are empty. D. walks fast. We reach the Gaumont, converted into a transit center. We ask for Hélène D., as arranged. She comes, she's laughing. I'm cold. Where are they? In the hotel. She takes us there.

The hotel. All the lights are on. People are coming and going, men in the striped uniforms of deportees and women assistants in white smocks. The arrivals go on all night. Here's the room; the assistant leaves us. I tell D., "Knock." My heart's leaping about, I'm not going to be able to go in. D. knocks. I go in with him. There are two people at the foot of a bed, a man and a woman. They don't say anything. They're relatives. In the bed there are two deportees. One's asleep, he looks about twenty. The other one smiles at me. I ask, "Are you Perrotti?" "Yes." "I'm Robert L.'s wife." "We last saw him two days ago." "How was he?" Perrotti looks at D. "There were some much more tired than he was." The young one has waked up. "Robert L.? Oh yes, we were supposed to escape together." I've seated myself near the bed. I ask, "Were they shooting people?" The two young men look at one another and don't answer right away. "Well, no . . . they'd stopped." D. speaks, "Are you sure?" Perrotti answers, "The day we left they hadn't shot anyone for two days." The two deportees talk among themselves. The young one asks, "How do you know?" "The Russian *kapo* told me." Me: "What did he say?" "That they'd been ordered not to do any more shooting." The young one: "There were some days when they shot people and other days when they didn't." Perrotti looks at me, looks at D., and smiles: "We're very tired, you must forgive us." D.'s eyes are riveted on Perrotti. "How is it he's not with you?" "We all looked for him before the train left, but we couldn't find him." "We did our best." "So how is it you didn't find him?" "It was dark," says Perrotti, "and there were still a lot of us." "You did look carefully?" "Well . . ." They glance at each other. "Yes," says the young one, "we looked. We even called out, though that was dangerous." "He was a good comrade," says Perrotti. "We looked for him all right. He gave lectures about France. You should have heard him talk—everyone was spellbound." Me: "If you didn't find him, wasn't it because he wasn't there? Because he'd been shot?" D. comes close to the bed, he's not polite any more, he's angry, he restrains himself, he's almost as pale as Perrotti. "When did you see him last?" The two look at each other. I can hear the woman saying, "They're tired." We're interrogating them as if they were criminals, we don't give them a moment's respite. "I saw him anyway," says the young one. "I'm sure of it." He stares into space and repeats that he's sure. But he isn't sure of anything. Nothing will stop D. "Try to remember—when did you see him last?" "I saw him in the column, don't you remember? On the right? It was still light . . . an hour before we reached the station." The young one: "God, we were tired . . . Anyway, I saw him after he escaped—I'm sure of it, because we even planned to get away together from the station." "What do you mean, 'he escaped'?" "Yes, he tried to escape, but he was caught." "But didn't they shoot those who tried to escape? You're not telling the truth." Perrotti can't tell us any more, his memory is in tatters, he's lost heart. "We've *told* you he'll come back, haven't we?" At this point D. breaks in vehemently. He tells me to be quiet and starts again. "When did he escape?" They look at each other. "Was it the day before?" "I think so." D. asks, begs, "Try, try . . . Forgive us . . . but try to remember!" Perrotti smiles. "I do understand, but we're so tired . . ." They don't say anything for a moment. Complete silence. Then the young one: "I'm sure I saw him after he escaped, I saw him in the column, now I'm sure." Perrotti: "When? How?" "With Girard, on the right, I'm sure." I ask again, "How did you know when they shot people?" Perrotti: "Don't worry, we'd have known, we always found out, the SS used to shoot people at the rear of the column, but the guys passed the word along to the front." D.: "What we'd like to know is why you didn't find him." "It was dark," says Perrotti again. "Perhaps he escaped again," says the young one. "Anyway, you saw him after he escaped the first time?" "Yes," says Perrotti, "that's absolutely certain." "What did they do to him?" "Well, they beat him up . . . Philippe will be able to tell you about that better than I can—they were pals." Me: "How was it they didn't shoot him?" "The Americans were so close they hadn't time." "And anyway it depended," says the young one. Me: "Was it *before* he escaped that you arranged to get away together at the station?" Silence. They look at one another. "You see," says D., "if you spoke to him *after*, it would be one more proof." No, they can't remember; about that they can't remember anything else. They can remember some of the movements of the column and the way some of their friends jumped into ditches to hide, and how there were Americans everywhere. But the rest, no, they can't remember.

Another period of torture begins. Germany is in flames. He's inside Germany. It's not quite certain. Not quite. But you can say this: if he hasn't been shot, if he stayed in the column, he's inside the conflagration that is Germany.

April 24
It's half-past eleven in the morning. The phone rings. I'm alone, it's I who answer it. It's François Mitterrand, known as Morland. "Philippe's back. He saw Robert a week ago. He was well." I explain, "I've seen Perrotti. Apparently Robert escaped and was caught. What does

Philippe know?" François: "Yes, he did try to escape. He was caught by some children." Me: "When did he see him last?" Silence. François: "They escaped together. Philippe had got some distance away and the Germans didn't see him. Robert was still near the road, he was beaten up. Philippe waited, but he didn't hear any shots." Silence. "Is that certain?" "Yes." "It's not much. Didn't he see him again afterward?" Silence. "No—Philippe had gone, he got away." "When was this?" "The thirteenth." I know François Morland has done all the calculations and made no mistakes. "So what are we to think?" "No question about it," says François, "he'll be back." Me: "Did they shoot people in the column?" Silence. "It depended. Come to the printer's." "No, I'm tired. What does Philippe think?" Silence. "No question about it, he should be here in forty-eight hours." Me: "How's Philippe?" "Very tired. He says Robert was still holding out. He was in better condition than Philippe." "Does he know anything about where the train was going?" "No, he has no idea." Me: "You're not just having me on?" "No. Come to the printer's." "No, I don't want to. Listen: what if he's not back in forty-eight hours?" "What do you expect me to say?" "Why did you say forty-eight hours, particularly?" "Because according to Philippe they were liberated between the fourteenth and the twenty-fifth. So that must be right."

Perrotti—escaped on the twelfth, back on the twenty-fourth. Philippe—escaped on the thirteenth, back on the twenty-fourth. You have to allow between ten and twelve days. Robert ought to be here tomorrow or the day after. Perhaps tomorrow.

Thursday, April 26

D. called the doctor, I still have a temperature. Madame Katz, mother of my friend Jeanine Katz, has come to live here while she waits for her daughter, who was deported to Ravensbrück with Marie-Louise, Robert's sister. Riby phoned and asked for Robert. He was in the column, he escaped before Perrotti, got back before him.

Friday, April 27

Nothing. Day or night. D. brings me *Combat*. In the final edition the Russians have captured a metro station in Berlin. But Zhukov's guns are still surrounding and pounding the ruins of Berlin, less than a hundred yards apart. Stettin and Brno have been taken. The Americans are on the Danube. All Germany is in their hands. It's difficult to occupy a country. What can they do with it? I've become like Madame Bordes, I don't get up any more. Madame Katz does the shopping and the cooking. She has a bad heart. She has bought me some American milk. I believe Madame Katz would think less about her daughter if I were really ill. Her daughter's a cripple, she had a stiff leg from tuberculosis of the bone; she was Jewish. I found out at the center that they killed cripples. We're starting to find out about the Jews. Madame Katz waited for six months, from April to November 1945. Her daughter had died in March 1945; it took nine months to trace the name. I don't speak to her about Robert L. She's left her daughter's description everywhere—at the centers, at all the frontiers, with all her family—you never know. She's bought fifty cans of American milk, twenty kilos of sugar, calcium, phosphate, alcohol, eau de Cologne, rice, potatoes. Madame Katz says (word for word), "All her underwear is washed and mended and ironed. I've had her black coat lined and the pockets seen to. I had everything in a big trunk with mothballs, but I've aired it, everything's ready. I've had new tips put on her shoes and darned her stockings. I don't think I've forgotten anything." Madame Katz is challenging God.

April 27

Nothing. The black hole. No light thrown. I go over the sequence of days, but there's a void, a gulf, between the time when Philippe didn't hear a shot and the station, where no one saw Robert. I get up. Madame Katz has gone to her son's place. I dress myself and sit down near the telephone. D. arrives. He insists on my going out for a meal with him. The restaurant is full. People are talking about the end of the war. I'm not hungry. Everyone's talking about German atrocities. I'm never hungry now. I'm nauseated by other people eating. I want to die. I'm cut off from the rest of the world by a razor; even from D. The hellish calculation: if I don't have any news by tonight, he's dead. D. looks at me. Well may he look at me, he's dead. Well might I say so, D. wouldn't believe me. *Pravda* says: "The twelfth hour has struck for Germany. The ring of fire and steel is tightening around Berlin." It's all over. He won't be there for the peace. The Italian partisans have captured Mussolini at Faenza. All northern Italy is in their hands. Mussolini has been captured, that's all anyone knows.

Thorez talks of the future, says we'll have to work. I've saved all the newspapers for Robert L. If he comes back, I'll eat with him. Before, no. I think of the German mother of the little sixteen-year-old soldier who lay dying on August 17, 1944, alone on a heap of stones on the quai des Arts; she's still waiting for her son. Now that de Gaulle's in power, now that he's become the man who for four years saved our honor, now that he's to be seen in broad daylight grudging the people their praise, there's something terrifying about him, awful. "So long as I'm there the firm will carry on," he says. He's not waiting now for anything but the peace; we're the only ones who are still waiting, in a suspense as old as time, that of women always, everywhere, waiting for the men to come home from the war. We belong to the part of the world where the dead pile up hugger-mugger in charnel houses. It's in Europe that this happens. That they burn Jews by the million. That they mourn them. America watches in amazement as the smoke rises from the crematoriums of Europe. I can't help thinking of the old gray-haired woman who'll be suffering and waiting for news of the son who died so alone, at sixteen, on the quai des Arts. Perhaps someone will have seen mine, the one I'm waiting for, just as I saw him, in a ditch, when his hands were making their last appeal and his eyes no longer could see. Someone who will never know what that man was to me; someone whose name I'll never know. We belong to Europe: it's here, in Europe, that we're shut up together confronting the rest of the world. Around us are the same oceans, the same invasions, the same wars. We are of the same race as those who were burned in the crematoriums, those who were gassed at Maïdenek; and we're also of the same race as the Nazis. They're great levelers, the crematoriums at Buchenwald, hunger, the common graves at Bergen-Belsen. We have a share in those graves; those strangely identical skeletons belong to one European family. It's not on an island in the Malay Archipelago or in some Pacific region that these things have happened, it's on our own soil, the soil of Europe. The four hundred thousand skeletons of the German Communists who died in Dora between 1933 and 1938 are in the great European common grave too, together with the millions of Jews and the idea of God —with every Jew, every one, the idea of God. The Americans say: "There isn't a single American now, not one barber in Chicago or farmer in Kentucky, who doesn't know what happened in the German concentration camps." The Americans mean to show us how well the American war machine works, how they've set at rest the misgivings of the farmer and the barber, who weren't sure before why their sons had been taken away from them to fight on the European front. When they're told about how Mussolini was executed and hung on butcher's hooks, they'll stop understanding and be shocked.

April 28
Those waiting for peace aren't waiting, not at all. There's less and less reason for not having any news. Peace is visible already. It's like a great darkness falling, it's the beginning of forgetting. You can see already:

Paris is lit up at night. The place Saint-Germain-des-Prés looks as if it's floodlit. The Café des Deux Magots is packed. It's still too cold for people to sit outside on the sidewalk. But the little restaurants are packed too. I went out, peace seemed imminent. I hurried back home, pursued by the peace. It had suddenly struck me that there might be a future, that a foreign land was going to emerge out of this chaos where no one would wait any more. There's no room for me here anywhere, I'm not here, I'm there with him in that region no one else can reach, no one else can know, where there's burning and killing. I'm hanging by a thread, by the last of all probabilities, for which there'll be no room in the papers. The lit-up city means only one thing to me: it is a sign of death, of a tomorrow without them. There's no present in the city now except for us who wait. For us it's a city *they* won't see. Everyone's impatient because peace is so slow in coming. What are they waiting for, why don't they sign the peace? You hear people saying it everywhere. The threat grows greater every day. Today we hear that Hitler is dying. Himmler said so on the German radio in a last appeal, offering to surrender to the Allies. Berlin is on fire, defended only by the "thirty suicide battalions," and in Berlin, Hitler is said to have blown his brains out. They say he's dead, but it's not certain.

April 28
The whole world is waiting. Himmler says, "Hitler is dying and will not survive the announcement of unconditional surrender." The shock would be fatal. The

United States and England have replied that they won't accept surrender unless the USSR is included too. Himmler sent his offer of capitulation to the San Francisco conference. At the last minute *Combat* announces that the offer of capitulation was addressed to Russia, too. The Stalinists don't want to hand Mussolini over to the Allies. The papers say he must expiate his crimes at the hands of the people. Farinacci has been tried by a people's tribunal and executed in a city square in the presence of a large crowd. Europe is having a difficult time in San Francisco, where it's in a minority. Stettinius is in the chair. *Combat* says: "When they see how the Great Powers behave, the smaller powers start to look up again." People are already talking about "after the peace."

There are an awful lot of them. There really are huge numbers of dead. Seven million Jews have been exterminated—transported in cattle cars, then gassed in specially built gas chambers, then burned in specially built ovens. In Paris, people don't talk about the Jews yet. Their infants were handed over to female officials responsible for the strangling of Jewish babies and experts in the art of killing by applying pressure on the carotid arteries. They smile and say it's painless. This new face of death that has been discovered in Germany —organized, rationalized—produces bewilderment before it arouses indignation. You're amazed. How can anyone still be a German? You look for parallels elsewhere and in other times, but there aren't any. Some people will always be overcome by it, inconsolable. One of the greatest civilized nations in the world, the age-long capital of music, has just systematically murdered eleven million human beings with the utter efficiency of a state industry. The whole world looks at the mountain, the mass of death dealt by God's creature to his fellows. Someone quotes the name of some German man of letters who's been very upset and become very depressed and to whom these things have given much food for thought. If Nazi crime is not seen in world terms, if it isn't understood collectively, then that man in the concentration camp at Belsen who died alone but with the same collective soul and class awareness that made him undo a bolt on the railroad one night somewhere in Europe, without a leader, without a uniform, without a witness, has been betrayed. If you give a German and not a collective interpretation to the Nazi horror, you reduce the man in Belsen to regional dimensions. The only possible answer to this crime is to turn it into a crime committed by everyone. To share it. Just like the idea of equality and fraternity. In order to bear it, to tolerate the idea of it, we must share the crime.

I can't remember what day it was, whether it was in April, no, it was a day in May when one morning at eleven o'clock the phone rang. It was from Germany, it was François Morland. He doesn't say hello, he's almost rough, but clear as always. "Listen carefully. Robert is alive. Now keep calm. He's in Dachau. Listen very, very carefully. Robert is very weak, so weak you can't imagine. I have to tell you—it's a question of hours. He may live for another three days like that, but no more. D. and Beauchamp must start out today, this morning, for Dachau. Tell them this: they're to go straight to my office—the people there will be expecting them. They'll be given French officers' uniforms, passports, mission orders, gasoline coupons, maps, and permits. Tell them to go right away. It's the only way. If they tried to do it officially they'd arrive too late."

François Morland and Rodin were part of a mission organized by Father Riquet. They had gone to Dachau, and that was where they'd found Robert L. They had gone into the prohibited area of the camp, where the dead and the hopeless cases were kept. And there, one of the latter had distinctly uttered a name: "François." "François," and then his eyes had closed again. It took Rodin and Morland an hour to recognize Robert L. Rodin finally identified him by his teeth. They wrapped him up in a sheet, as people wrap up a dead body, and took him out of the prohibited part of the camp and laid him down by a hut in the survivors' part of the camp. They were able to do so because there were no American soldiers around. They were all in the guard-room, scared of the typhus.

Beauchamp and D. left Paris the same day, early in the afternoon. It was May 12, the day of the peace. Beauchamp was wearing a colonel's uniform belonging to François Morland. D. was dressed as a lieutenant in the French army and carried his papers as a member of the Resistance, made out in the name of D. Masse. They drove all night and arrived at Dachau the next morning. They spent several hours looking for Robert L.; then, as they were going past a body, they heard someone say D.'s name. It's my opinion they didn't recognize him; but Morland had warned us he was unrecognizable. They took him. And it was only afterward they must have recognized him. Under their clothes they had a third French officer's uniform. They had to hold him upright, he could no longer stand alone, but they managed to dress him. They had to prevent him from saluting outside the SS huts, get him through the guard posts, see that he wasn't given any of the vaccinations that would have killed him. The American soldiers, blacks for the most part, wore gas masks against typhus, the fear was so great. Their orders were such that if they'd suspected the state Robert L. was really in, they'd have put him back immediately in the part of the camp where people were left to die. Once they got Robert L. out, the other two had to get him to walk to the Citroën II. As soon as they'd stretched him out on the back seat, he fainted. They thought it was all over, but no. The journey was very difficult, very slow. They had to stop every half hour because of the dysentery. As soon as they'd left Dachau behind, Robert L. spoke. He said he knew he wouldn't reach Paris alive. So he began to talk, so it should be told before he died. He didn't accuse any person, any race, any people. He accused man. Emerging from the horror, dying, delirious, Robert L. was still able not to accuse anyone except the governments that come and go in the history of nations. He wanted D. and Beauchamp to tell me after his death what he had said. They reached the French frontier that night, near Wissemburg. D. phoned me: "We've reached France. We've just crossed the frontier. We'll be back tomorrow by the end of the morning. Expect the worst. You won't recognize him." They had dinner in an officers' mess. Robert L. was still talking and telling his story. When he entered the mess all the officers stood up and saluted him. He didn't see. He never had seen that sort of thing. He spoke of the German martyrdom, of the martyrdom common to all men. He told what it was like. That evening he said he'd like to eat a trout before he died. In deserted Wissemburg they found a trout for Robert L. He ate a few mouthfuls. Then he started talking again. He spoke of charity. He'd heard some rhetorical phrases of Father Riquet's, and he started to say these very obscure words: "When anyone talks to me of Christian charity, I shall say Dachau." But he didn't finish. That night they slept somewhere near Bar-sur-Aube. Robert L. slept for a few hours. They reached Paris at the end of the morning. Just before they came to the rue Saint-Benoît, D. stopped to phone me again: "I'm ringing to warn you that it's more terrible than anything we've imagined . . . He's happy."

I heard stifled cries on the stairs, a stir, a clatter of feet. Then doors banging and shouts. It was them. It was them, back from Germany.

I couldn't stop myself—I started to run downstairs, to escape into the street. Beauchamp and D. were supporting him under the arms. They'd stopped on the first-floor landing. He was looking up.

I can't remember exactly what happened. He must have looked at me and recognized me and smiled. I shrieked no, that I didn't want to see. I started to run again, up the stairs this time. I was shrieking, I remember that. The war emerged in my shrieks. Six years without uttering a cry. I found myself in some neighbors' apartment. They forced me to drink some rum, they poured it into my mouth. Into the shrieks.

I can't remember when I found myself back with him again, with him, Robert L. I remember hearing sobs all over the house; that the tenants stayed for a long while out on the stairs; that the doors were left open. I was told later that the concierge had put decorations up in the hall to welcome him, and that as soon as he'd gone by she tore them all down and shut herself up alone in her lodge to weep.

In my memory, at a certain moment, the sounds stop and I see him. Huge. There before me. I don't recognize him. He looks at me. He smiles. Lets himself be looked at. There's a supernatural weariness in his smile, weariness from having managed to live till this moment. It's from this smile that I suddenly recognize him, but from a great distance, as if I were seeing him at the other end of a tunnel. It's a smile of embarrassment. He's apologizing for being here, reduced to such a wreck. And then the smile fades, and he becomes a stranger again. But the knowledge is still there, that this stranger is he, Robert L., totally.

He wanted to see around the apartment again. We supported him, and he toured the rooms. His cheeks creased, but didn't release his lips; it was in his eyes that we'd seen his smile. In the kitchen he saw the clafoutis we'd made for him. He stopped smiling.

"What is it?" We told him. What was it made with? Cherries—it was the height of the season. "May I have some?" "We don't know, we'll have to ask the doctor." He came back into the sitting room and lay down on the divan. "So I can't have any?" "Not yet." "Why?" "There have been accidents in Paris already from letting deportees eat too soon after they got back from the camps."

He stopped asking questions about what had happened while he was away. He stopped seeing us. A great, silent pain spread over his face because he was still being refused food, because it was still as it had been in the concentration camp. And, as in the camp, he accepted it in silence. He didn't see that we were weeping. Nor did he see that we could scarcely look at him or respond to what he said.

The doctor came. He stopped short with his hand on the door handle, very pale. He looked at us, and then at the form on the divan. He didn't understand. And then he realized: the form wasn't dead yet, it was hovering between life and death, and he, the doctor, had been called in to try to keep it alive. The doctor came into the room. He went over to the form and the form smiled at him. The doctor was to come several times a day for three weeks, at all hours of the day and night. Whenever we were too afraid we called him and he came. He saved Robert L. He too was caught up in the passionate desire to save Robert L. from death. He succeeded.

We smuggled the clafoutis out of the house while he

slept. The next day he was feverish and didn't talk about food any more.

If he had eaten when he got back from the camp his stomach would have been lacerated by the weight of the food, or else the weight would have pressed on the heart, which had grown enormous in the cave of his emaciation. It was beating so fast you couldn't have counted its beats, you couldn't really say it was beating —it was trembling, rather, as if from terror. No, he couldn't eat without dying. But he couldn't go on not eating without dying. That was the problem.

The fight with death started very soon. We had to be careful with it, use care, tact, skill. It surrounded him on all sides. And yet there was still a way of reaching him. It wasn't very big, this opening through which to communicate with him, but there was still life in him, scarcely more than a splinter, but a splinter just the same. Death unleashed its attack. His temperature was 104.5° the first day. Then 105°. Then 106°. Death was doing all it could. 106°: his heart vibrated like a violin string. Still 106°, but vibrating. The heart, we thought—it's going to stop. Still 106°. Death deals cruel knocks, but the heart is deaf. This can't go on, the heart will stop. But no.

Gruel, said the doctor, a teaspoonful at a time. Six or seven times a day we gave him gruel. Just a teaspoonful nearly choked him, he clung to our hands, gasped for air, and fell back on the bed. But he swallowed some. Six or seven times a day, too, he asked to go to the toilet. We lifted him up, supported him under the arms and knees. He must have weighed between eighty-two and eighty-four pounds: bone, skin, liver, intestines, brain, lungs, everything—eighty-four pounds for a body five feet ten inches tall. We sat him on the edge of the sanitary pail, on which we'd put a small cushion: the skin was raw where there was no flesh between it and the joints. (*The elbows of the little Jewish girl of seventeen from the Faubourg du Temple stick through the skin on her arms. Probably because she's so young and her skin so fragile, the joint is outside instead of in, sticking out naked and clean. She suffers no pain either from her joints or from her belly, from which all her genital organs have been taken out one by one at regular intervals.*) Once he was sitting on his pail he excreted in one go, in one enormous, astonishing gurgle. What the heart held back the anus couldn't: it let out all that was in it. Everything, or almost everything, did the same, even the fingers, which no longer kept their nails, but let them go too. But the heart went on holding back what it contained. The heart. And then there was the head. Gaunt but sublime, it emerged alone from that bag of bones, remembering, relating, recognizing, asking for things. And talking. Talking. The head was connected to the body by the neck, as heads usually are, but the neck was so withered and shrunken—you could circle it with one hand—that you wondered how life could pass through it; a spoonful of gruel almost blocked it. At first the neck was at right angles to the shoulders. Higher up, the neck was right inside the skeleton, joined on at the top of the jaws and winding around the ligaments like ivy. You could see the vertebrae through it, the carotid arteries, the nerves, the pharynx, and the blood passing through: the skin had become like cigarette paper. So, he excreted this dark green, slimy, gushing thing, a turd such as no one had ever seen before. When he'd finished we put him back to bed. He lay for a long time with his eyes half shut, prostrated.

For seventeen days the turd looked the same. It was inhuman. It separated him from us more than the fever, the thinness, the nailless fingers, the marks of SS blows. We gave him gruel that was golden yellow, gruel for infants, and it came out of him dark green like slime from a swamp. After the sanitary pail was closed you could hear the bubbles bursting as they rose to the surface inside. Viscous and slimy, it was almost like a great gob of spit. When it emerged the room filled with a smell, not of putrefaction or corpses—did his body still have the wherewithal to make a corpse?— but rather of humus, of dead leaves, of dense undergrowth. It was a somber smell, dark reflection of the dark night from which he was emerging and which we would never know. (*I leaned against the shutters, the street went by below, and as they didn't know what was going on in the room I wanted to tell them that here, in this room above them, a man had come back from the German camps, alive.*)

Of course he'd rummaged in trashcans for food, he'd eaten wild plants, drunk water from engines. But that didn't explain it. Faced with this strange phenomenon we tried to find explanations. We thought that perhaps there, under our very eyes, he was consuming his own liver or spleen. How were we to know? How were we to know what strangeness that belly still contained, what pain?

For seventeen whole days that turd still looks the same. For seventeen days it's unlike anything ever known. Every one of the seven times he excretes each day, we smell it, look at it, but can't recognize it. For seventeen days we hide from him that which comes out of him, just as we hide from him his own legs and feet and whole unbelievable body.

We ourselves never got used to seeing them. You couldn't get used to it. The incredible thing was that he was still alive. Whenever anyone came into the room and saw that shape under the sheets, they couldn't bear the sight and averted their eyes. Many went away and never came back. He never noticed our horror, not once. He was happy, he wasn't afraid any more. The fever bore him up. For seventeen days.

One day his temperature drops.

After seventeen days, death grows weary. In the pail his excretion doesn't bubble any more, it becomes liquid. It's still green, but it smells more human, it smells human. And one day his temperature drops— he's been given twelve liters of serum, and one morning his temperature drops. He's lying on his nine cushions, one for the head, two for the forearms, two for the arms, two for the hands, and two for the feet. For no part of his body could bear its own weight; the weight had to be swathed in down and immobilized.

And then, one morning, the fever leaves him. It comes back, but abates again. Comes back again, not quite so high, and falls again. And then one morning he says, "I'm hungry."

Hunger had gone as his temperature rose. It came back when the fever abated. One day the doctor said, "Let's try—let's try giving him something to eat. We can begin with meat extract. If he can take that, keep on giving it, but at the same time give him all kinds of other food, just small amounts at first, increasing the quantity just a little every three days."

I spend the morning going around to all the restaurants in Saint-Germain-des-Prés trying to find a meat-juice extractor. I find one in a fashionable restaurant. They say they can't lend it. I say it's for a political deportee who's very ill, it's a matter of life and death. The woman thinks for a minute and says, "I can't lend it to you, but I can rent it to you for a thousand francs a day." I leave my name and address and a deposit. The Saint-Benoît restaurant sells me the meat at cost price.

He digested the meat extract without any difficulty, so after three days he began to take solid food.

His hunger grew from what it fed on. It grew greater and greater, became insatiable.

It took on terrifying proportions.

We didn't serve him food. We put the dishes in front of him and left him and he ate. Methodically, as if performing a duty, he was doing what he had to do to live. He ate. It was an occupation that took up all his time. He would wait for food for hours. He would swallow without knowing what he was eating. Then we'd take the food away and he'd wait for it to come again.

He has gone and hunger has taken his place. Emptiness has taken his place. He is giving to the void, filling what was emptied: those wasted bowels. That's what he's doing. Obeying, serving, ministering to a mysterious duty. How does he know what to do about hunger? How does he perceive that this is what he has to do? He knows with a knowledge that has no parallel.

He eats a mutton chop. Then he gnaws the bone, eyes lowered, concentrating on not missing a morsel of meat. Then he takes a second chop. Then a third. Without looking up.

He's sitting in the shade in the sitting room near a half-open window, in an armchair, surrounded by his cushions, his stick beside him. His legs look like crutches inside his trousers. When the sun shines you can see through his hands.

Yesterday he made enormous efforts to gather up the breadcrumbs that had fallen on his trousers and on the floor. Today he lets a few lie.

We leave him alone in the room while he's eating. We don't have to help him now. His strength has come back enough for him to hold a spoon or a fork. But we still cut up the meat for him. We leave him alone with the food. We try not to talk in the adjoining rooms. We walk on tiptoe. We watch him from a distance. He's performing a duty. He has no special preference for one dish over another. He cares less and less. He crams everything down. If the dishes don't come fast enough, he sobs and says we don't understand.

Yesterday afternoon he stole some bread out of the refrigerator. He steals. We tell him to be careful, not to eat too much. Then he weeps.

I used to watch him from the sitting-room door. I didn't go in. For two weeks, three, I watched him eat with unremitting pleasure. I couldn't get used to it either. Sometimes his pleasure made me weep too. He didn't see me. He'd forgotten me.

Strength is coming back.

I start to eat again too, and to sleep. I put on some weight. We're going to live. Like him I haven't been able to eat for seventeen days. Like him I haven't slept for seventeen days, or at least that's what I think. In fact, I've slept for two or three hours a day. I fall asleep anywhere. And wake in terror. It's awful, every time I think he's died while I was asleep. I still have that slight fever at night. The doctor who comes to see him is worried about me, too. He prescribes injections. The needle breaks in the muscle in my thigh, my muscles are knotted, as if tetanized. The nurse won't give me any more injections. Lack of sleep gives me eye trouble. I have to hold on to the furniture when I walk, the ground seems to slope away from me, I'm afraid of falling. We eat the meat from which we extracted the juice. It's like paper or cotton wool. I don't cook any more, except coffee. I feel very close to the death I wished for. It's a matter of indifference to me; I don't even think about it's being a matter of indifference. My identity has gone. I'm just she who is afraid when she wakes. She who wills in his stead, for him. I exist in that will, that desire, and even when Robert L. is at death's door it's inexpressibly strong because he is still alive. When I lost my younger brother and my baby I lost pain too. It was without an object, so to speak: it was built on the past. But now there is hope, and pain is implanted in hope. Sometimes I'm amazed I don't die; a cold blade plunged deep into the living flesh, night and day, and you survive.

Strength is coming back.

We were informed by telephone. For a month we kept the news from him. It was only after he'd got some of his strength back, while he was staying at Verrières-le-Buisson at a convalescent home for deportees, that we told him of the death of his younger sister, Marie-Louise L. It was at night. His youngest sister and I were there. We said, "There's something we've been keeping from you." He said, "Marie-Louise is dead." We stayed together in the room till daylight, without speaking about her, without speaking. I vomited. I think we all did. He kept saying, "Twenty-four years old." Sitting on the bed, his hands on his stick, not weeping.

More strength came back. Another day I told him we had to get a divorce, that I wanted a child by D., that it was because of the name the child would bear. He asked if one day we might get together again. I said no, that I hadn't changed my mind since two years ago, since I'd met D. I said that even if D. hadn't existed I wouldn't have lived with him again. He didn't ask me my reasons for leaving. I didn't tell him what they were.

One time we're at Saint-Jorioz on Lake Annecy, in a rest home for deportees. It's a roadside hotel with a restaurant attached. It's in August 1945. It's there we hear about Hiroshima. He's got some of his weight back. But he hasn't the strength to carry it. He walks with that stick: I can see it now, a thick stick, made of some dark wood. Sometimes it's as if he'd like to lash out with it, hit walls, furniture, doors—not people, no, but all the things he meets. D. is there by Lake Annecy too. We haven't any money to go to hotels where we'd have to pay.

I don't see him as near to us during that trip to Savoy. He's surrounded by strangers, he's still alone, he doesn't say what he's thinking. He's hidden. He's dark. Then by the side of the road one morning that huge headline: Hiroshima.

It's as if he'd like to lash out, as if he's blinded by a rage through which he has to pass before he can live again. After Hiroshima I think he talks to D. D. is his best friend, Hiroshima is perhaps the first thing outside his own life that he sees or reads about.

Another time, it was before Savoy, he was standing among the tables outside the Café Flore. It was very sunny. He wanted to go to the Flore "to see," he said. The waiters came up and greeted him. And it's at that moment that I see him now, shouting, banging on the ground with his stick. I'm afraid he's going to smash the windows. The waiters look at him in consternation, almost in tears, speechless. And then I see him sit down, and sit there for a long while in silence.

Then more time went by.

It was the first summer of the peace—1946.

It was a beach in Italy, between Leghorn and La Spezia.

A year and four months have gone by since he came back from the camps. He's known about his sister, he's known about our separation, for many months.

He's there, on the beach, he's watching some people approach. I don't know who. The way he looked at things, his way of seeing—that was what died first in the German image of his death I had while I was waiting for him in Paris. Sometimes he stays a long while without saying anything, looking at the ground. He still can't get used to the death of his younger sister: twenty-four years old, blind, her feet frostbitten, in the last stages of consumption, flown from Ravensbrück to Copenhagen and dead on the day she arrived, the day of the armistice. He never mentions her, never utters her name.

He wrote a book on what he thought he had experienced in Germany. It was called *The Human Race*. Once the book was written, finished, published, he never spoke of the German concentration camps again. Never uttered the words again. Never again. Nor the title of the book.

· · ·

It's a day when the *libeccio*, the southwest wind, is blowing.

In the light that goes with the wind, the idea that he's dead ends.

I'm lying down beside Ginetta. We've climbed up the slope from the beach and gone deep in among the reeds. We've undressed. We've just emerged from the coolness of our swim; the sun blazes down on the coolness without yet reaching it. The skin offers good protection. On my skin, beneath my ribs, in a hollow, I can see my heart beating. I'm hungry.

The others have stayed on the beach. They're playing football. All except Robert L. Not yet.

Above the reeds you can see the snowy sides of the marble quarries of Carrara. Above them are higher mountains, sparkling white. Nearer, on the other side, you can see Mount Marcello, just over the estuary of La Magra. You can't see the village of Mount Marcello, only the hill, the groves of fig trees, and right at the top the dark sides of the pines.

We can hear them; they're laughing. Especially Elio. Ginetta says, "Listen to him—he's like a child."

Robert L. isn't laughing. He's lying under an umbrella. He still can't bear the sun. He watches the others playing.

The wind can't get through the reeds, but it brings us the sounds from the beach. It's terribly hot.

Ginetta takes two halves of lemon out of her bathing cap and gives me one. We squeeze the lemon over our open mouths. It runs down our throats drop by drop, reaches our hunger, and makes us feel its depth and strength. Ginetta says lemon is the fruit you need when it's as hot as this. She says, "Look at the lemons on the plain around Carrara—see how huge they are, they've got thick skins that keep them cool in the sun, they have as much juice as oranges, but they've got a harsh taste."

We can still hear the players. But Robert L.—we still can't hear him. It's in that silence that the war's still there, flowing across the sand and through the wind.

Ginetta says, "I'm sorry I didn't know you when you were waiting for Robert to come back." She says she thinks he looks well, but as if he tires easily. She notices it especially when he walks or swims, from his slowness, his painful slowness. But as she didn't know him before, she says she can't be sure. But she's afraid he may never be as strong again as he was before the camps.

At the name, Robert L., I weep. I still weep. I shall weep all my life. Ginetta apologizes and is silent.

Every day she thinks I'm going to be able to talk about him, and still I can't. But that day I tell her I think I shall be able to one day. And that I've already written something about that return. Tried to say something about that love. That it was then, by his deathbed, that I knew him, Robert L., best, that I understood forever what made him himself, himself alone and nothing and no one else in the world. Then I spoke of Robert L.'s special grace here below, of his own peculiar grace which carried him through the camps—the intelligence, the love, the reading, the politics, and all the inexpressible things of all the days; that grace peculiar to him but made up equally of the despair of all.

The heat became too unbearable. We put on our swim-suits again and ran down across the beach and straight into the sea. Ginetta swam far out. I stayed near the shore.

The *libeccio* had stopped blowing. Or else it was another day with no wind.

Or else it was another year. Another summer. Another day with no wind.

The sea was blue, even there before our eyes, and there weren't any waves, just a very gentle swell, a breath in a deep sleep. The others stopped playing and squatted down on their towels in the sand. He stood up and walked over to the sea. I came near the edge. I looked at him. He saw me looking. He blinked his eyes behind his glasses and smiled at me, giving little shakes of his head, as you do when you're laughing at someone. And I knew he knew, knew that every hour of every day I was thinking, "He didn't die in the concentration camp."

MONSIEUR X, HERE
CALLED PIERRE RABIER

This is a true story, right down to the details. It's out of consideration for the wife and child of the man here referred to as Rabier that I haven't published it before, and that even now I take the precaution of not using his real name. Now the facts lie buried under forty years, everyone is old, and even if they learn about those facts for the first time, they won't be wounded by them as they would have been before, when everyone was young.

Still, it might be asked: why publish now something that is in a way merely anecdotal? Admittedly it was true, and terrifying to live through, enough to make you die of horror. But that was all; it never became anything greater, never took off into literature. So?

Still hesitating, I wrote it. Still hesitating, I showed it to my friends Hervé Lemasson and Yann Andréa. They decided it ought to be published because of the description of Rabier, and of his illusion that a person may exist solely as a dispenser of reward and punishment. An illusion that usually takes the place of ethics, philosophy, and morality—and not only in the police.

It is the morning of June 6, 1944, in the main waiting room of the prison at Fresnes.* I've come to bring a parcel for my husband, who was arrested on June 1, six days ago. There's an air-raid alert, and the Germans shut the doors of the waiting room and leave us there alone. There are ten or so of us. We don't talk to each other. The sound of the planes arrives over Paris; it's enormous. I hear someone telling me, in a low but clear voice, "They landed this morning at six o'clock." I turn around. It's a young man. I cry out, but quietly, "It's not true—don't spread false news!" The young man says, "It *is* true." We don't believe him. Everyone weeps. The alert is over and the Germans turn everyone out of the waiting room. No parcels today. It's when I'm back in Paris—in the rue de Rennes —that I see: all the faces around me, looking at each other dumbfounded, smiling. I stop a young man and ask, "Is it true?" He says, "Yes."

Food parcels are suspended indefinitely. I go to Fresnes several times in vain. Then I decide to get a parcel permit through the rue des Saussaies. One of my friends who's a secretary at the Ministry of Information undertakes to phone Dr. Kieffer (avenue Foch) in the

* The Germans turned Fresnes, on the outskirts of Paris, into a camp for political prisoners.

name of her director to get a recommendation for a permit. They ask her to go there. She's seen by Dr. Kieffer's secretary, a man, who tells her the place to go is room 415 E4 on the fourth floor of the old building in the rue des Saussaies. No letter of recommendation. I wait several days outside the ministry in the rue des Saussaies. The line stretches for a hundred yards along the sidewalk. We wait, not to enter the offices of the German police, but to take our turn to be able to enter. Three days. Four days. I can only mention Dr. Kieffer's recommendation to the secretary in the office of parcel permits. First I have to go to room 415 and see a certain Monsieur Hermann. I wait all morning. Monsieur Hermann isn't in. The secretary in a nearby office, a woman, gives me a note allowing me to come back next morning. Once again Monsieur Hermann isn't in and I wait all morning. The landing was a week ago now and you sense demoralization in the upper echelons of the German police. My pass expires at midday. I search in vain for the secretary I saw the day before. I go up to a tall man in the corridor and ask him to be good enough to extend my pass till the evening. He asks to see my card. I give it to him. He says, "But this is the business of the rue Dupin."

He mentions my husband's name. He tells me it was he who arrested him. And he who was the first to question him. This is Monsieur X., here called Pierre Rabier, an agent of the Gestapo.

"Are you a relation?"

"I'm his wife."

"Oh . . . It's a bothersome business, this . . ."

I don't ask Pierre Rabier any questions. He is extremely polite. He renews my pass himself. And he tells me Hermann will be there tomorrow.

I see Rabier again the next day when I come to see Hermann for the parcel permit. As I'm waiting in the corridor he comes out of a door. He's holding a woman in his arms, she's half fainting and very pale, her clothes are drenched. He smiles at me and disappears. He comes back a few minutes later and smiles again.

"Still waiting . . . ?"

I say it doesn't matter. He brings up the rue Dupin again.

"A real barracks of a place. . . . And there was this map on the table . . . It's quite a serious matter."

He asks me some questions. Did I know my husband belonged to a Resistance organization? Did I know the people who lived in the rue Dupin? I say I didn't know most of them very well and didn't know others at all, that I wrote books and wasn't interested in anything else. He says he knows, my husband told him. He even found two of my novels on the table in the sitting room when he arrested him. He laughs. He even took them away with him. He doesn't ask me any more questions. Finally he tells me the truth, that I can't get a parcel permit because parcel permits have been abolished. But it's still possible to get parcels through via the German examining officer when he interrogates the prisoners.

The examining officer is Hermann, the one I've been waiting to see for three days. He comes late in the afternoon. I mention the solution suggested by Rabier. He says I can't see my husband, but that he'll see to it that he and his sister get the parcels. I can bring them the next morning. As I'm leaving Hermann's office I meet Rabier again. He smiles, offers comfort: my husband isn't going to be shot "despite the plan to blow up German installations that was found on the table with the two novels." He laughs.

I live in total isolation. My only link with the outside world is a phone call from D. every morning and evening.

Three weeks go by. The Gestapo haven't come to search my apartment. Given the present situation, we think they won't come now. I ask to be allowed to start work again. I get permission. François Morland, the head of our movement, needs a liaison officer and asks through a third party if I'll replace Ferry, who's going to Toulouse. I agree.

At eleven-thirty in the morning on the first Monday in July I'm to establish contact between Duponceau (at that time the MNPGD's* delegate in Switzerland) and Godard (chief secretary to Henri Frenay, minister for prisoners). We're to meet at the corner of the boulevard Saint-Germain opposite the Chamber of Deputies. I get there on time. Duponceau is there, I go up to him, and we talk with the easy, natural air that members of the Resistance affect in broad daylight. Before five minutes have passed I hear someone calling me from a few yards away: Pierre Rabier. He snaps his fingers as

* MNPDG: Mouvement National des Prisonniers de Guerre et Déportés (National Movement for Prisoners of War and Deportees).

he calls me, his expression is severe. I think we're lost. I say to Duponceau, "It's the Gestapo—we've had it." I go over to Rabier without showing any hesitation. He doesn't say good morning.

"Do you recognize me?"

"Yes."

"Where did you see me before?"

"In the rue des Saussaies."

Either he's here by pure chance or he's come to arrest us. In the latter case the police car is waiting around the corner and it's already too late.

I smile at Rabier. I say, "I'm very glad I've run into you—I've tried several times to see you, coming out of the rue des Saussaies. I haven't had any news about my husband . . ." His severe expression fades at once, though this doesn't reassure me. He's cheerful, cordial, gives me news of my sister-in-law, whom he's seen and given the parcel Hermann took charge of. He hasn't seen my husband, but knows he got the parcel. I can't remember anything else he said. But I do remember this: on the one hand, Duponceau, so as not to lose me—and "lose contact"—stays where he is; and on the other hand, Godard arrives and by some miracle doesn't come over to me. Every moment I expect him to mistake Rabier for Duponceau and come over and shake hands. But he doesn't. We, Rabier and I, are sandwiched between two of my colleagues, one five yards in front and the other five yards behind. This classic comic situation doesn't make anyone laugh. Even today I still wonder how it was that Rabier didn't notice my agitation. I must have been green in the face. I set my jaws to pre-

vent my teeth chattering. Apparently Rabier doesn't
notice. For ten minutes he goes on talking. I don't hear
a word. Apparently he doesn't care. As time goes by a
hope starts to glimmer through my fear: perhaps I'm
dealing with a madman. Because of Rabier's subse-
quent behavior I've never quite abandoned this impression. As he speaks, people go by and stop quite near us:
Madame Bigorrie and her son, neighbors from my own
quarter that I haven't seen for ten years. I can't say a
word. They hurry away, probably appalled at how
much I've changed. Rabier says, "You do know a lot
of people around here!"—later on he often referred to
all those we met that day—then goes on talking. I hear
him say he'll soon have some information about my
husband. I immediately play along with him, as I often
did later, and insist on seeing him again, on making an
appointment. He gives me one for the same evening at
half-past five in the gardens in the avenue Marigny.
We separate. Slowly I rejoin Duponceau; I say I don't
understand. Rabier's colleague must be around the corner. I'm still horribly confused, because I simply can't
understand why Rabier called me over, nor why he
kept me talking so long. No one comes from around
the corner. I indicate to Duponceau that the man over
there, three yards away, is the one he is to contact.
Godard. I leave, not having the least idea what's going
to happen. I don't know if I did right in not warning
Godard myself. I don't look back. I go straight to the
offices of Gallimard, the publishers. I collapse into a
chair. I find out that night: my colleagues weren't arrested.

· · ·

Rabier really was there by chance. He had stopped because he recognized the French girl who'd brought the parcel to the rue des Saussaies. I found this out afterward. Rabier was fascinated by French intellectuals, artists, authors. He'd gone into the Gestapo because he hadn't been able to buy an art bookshop.

I see Rabier that evening. He hasn't any news for me, either about my husband or about my sister-in-law. But he says he might have.

From then on Rabier phones me, at first every other day, then every day. Soon he asks me to meet him. I do. François Morland has issued strict orders: I'm to maintain this contact, the only one that still connects us to our comrades who've been arrested. And if I stopped keeping my appointments with Rabier, he'd start to suspect me.

I see Rabier every day. Sometimes he invites me to lunch, always in black market restaurants. Usually we go to cafés. He tells me about the arrests he's made. But above all he tells me not about his present life but about the life he'd like to have. The little art bookshop is often mentioned. I make sure every time to remind him about my husband. He says he's bearing him in mind. Despite François Morland's orders, I try several times to break with Rabier, but I warn him, I say I'm going to the country, I'm tired. He doesn't believe me. He doesn't know if I'm innocent or not; he does know he has me in his power. He's right. I never do go to the country. There's always the insurmountable fear of being cut off for good from Robert L., my husband. I keep saying I want to know where he is. Rabier swears he's looking into it. He says he's saved him from being put on trial and that he's now being treated like the people who resist forced labor, the STO. But I have him in my power, too. If I find out that my husband's been sent to Germany I won't need to see him any more, and he knows this. The story about the STO is untrue, as I learn later. But if Rabier tells lies it's to reassure me. I'm sure he thinks he can do much more than he really can. I think he even imagined he could arrange for my husband to come back, just so as to be able to keep hold of me. But the main thing is that he must not tell me my husband has been shot because they no longer know what to do with the prisoners.

Again I'm almost totally isolated. The orders are that no one is to come to my place or to recognize me on any account. Of course I drop all other duties. I get very thin, until I weigh the same as a deportee. Every day I expect Rabier to arrest me. Every day I tell my concierge "for the last time" where I'm meeting Rabier and what time I should be home. I see only one of my colleagues, D., known as Masse, second in command to Captain Rodin, commando leader and managing editor of the newspaper *L'Homme Libre*. We meet a long way from where we live, walking through the streets and parks. I tell him what I've found out from Rabier.

A split develops in the movement.
Some want to kill Rabier at once.
Others want me to leave Paris, fast.

In a letter that D. arranges to have conveyed to François Morland, I promise on my honor to do all I can to help the movement kill Rabier before the police get hold of him, just as soon as I know my husband and sister-in-law are out of his reach. In other words, out of France. For on top of the other dangers there's this: Rabier might find out that I belong to a Resistance movement, and this might make things worse for Robert L.

My relationship with Rabier falls into two distinct phases.

The first starts when I meet him in a corridor in the rue des Saussaies and ends with my letter to François Morland. It's a period of fear—daily, awful, overwhelming fear.

The second phase lasts from the letter to François Morland up to Rabier's arrest. It's a period full of the same fear, it's true, but of a fear that sometimes turns into relish at having settled that he must die. At having defeated him on his own ground: death.

My appointments with Rabier are always made at the last minute, in odd places and at odd times, such as twenty to six or ten past four. Sometimes he arranges to meet me in the street, sometimes in a café. But whether it's in the street or in a café, Rabier always gets there long before the appointed time and waits some distance away. When we're to meet in a café, he may be on the other side of the street; when we're to meet in the street, he's always some way away from the actual place. He's always in the place where you get the best view of the person you're waiting for. Often when I arrive I can't see him, and he appears from somewhere behind me. But often when I arrive I do see him; he's a hundred yards away from the café where we're supposed to meet, with his bicycle propped up beside him against a wall or a lamppost, and his briefcase in his hand.

Every evening I write down what happened when I saw Rabier, what I heard, true or false, about the trainloads of deportees being sent to Germany, about news from the front, about the starvation in Paris—there's really nothing left, we're cut off from Normandy, off which Paris has lived for five years. I take these notes to give to Robert L. when he comes back. I also have an ordnance survey map on which, day after day, I plot the advance of the Allied armies in Normandy and toward Germany. I keep the newspapers.

Logically, Rabier ought to do all he can to remove from Paris the best witness to his activity in the Gestapo, the most credible and the most dangerous witness against him: a writer, the wife of a member of the Resistance. Me. But he doesn't.

He always gives me information, even when he doesn't realize it. Generally, it's just backstairs gossip from the rue des Saussaies. But that's how I find out that the Germans are starting to get frightened, that some of them are deserting, and that transport is their most difficult problem.

François Morland too is beginning to be nervous. As for D., he's been nervous since the very first day. About Monsieur Leroy. Me.

I forgot to say that Rabier always arranges to meet me in open places with several exits: at corner cafés or intersections. The districts he likes best are the sixth arrondissement, Saint-Lazare, the République, Duroc.

At first I was afraid he'd ask to come up for a moment after seeing me back to my door. But he never did. I know he thought of it as early as our first rendezvous in the park in the avenue Marigny.

The last time I saw Rabier he asked me to go and have a drink with him "in the studio of a friend who was out of Paris." I said, "Some other time," and escaped. But he knew that was the last time. He'd already decided to leave Paris that evening. What he wasn't sure of was what he would have done with me, how he would have seduced me, whether he would have taken me with him when he ran away, or if he would have killed me.

I've just remembered that he was caught once before, in the rue des Renaudes, in a studio he occupied under his own name, I believe. And then he was released. And I remember that twenty years later it was in that same street that Georges Figon* was found, allegedly having committed suicide, by the French police. It's a street I don't know. The name's dark, blind, like that of a last hiding place.

Only once did I see him in a bad way, with his brown jacket splitting at the armholes and buttons missing. He had cuts and bruises on his face. His shirt was torn. It was in one of the last cafés along the rue de Sèvres, at Duroc. He was exhausted, but he smiled amiably as usual.

"They got away. There were too many of them."

He corrected himself: "It was tough, they fought, there were six of them, around the pool in the Luxembourg Gardens. They were young, and could run faster than I could."

He felt a pang, no doubt, like a rejected lover. He gave a sad smile. He'd soon be too old to arrest young men.

I think that was the day he spoke about the informers that all Resistance movements inevitably produce. It was he who told me we'd been betrayed by a member of our own network. He had been arrested, and had talked under the threat of deportation. Rabier said, "It was easy—he told us where it was, which room, which

---

* Georges Figon: A journalist involved in the Ben Barka affair. Ben Barka, a left-wing Moroccan opposition leader who had taken refuge in France, was abducted from outside a restaurant in Saint-Germain-des-Prés in Paris, and presumably murdered, in the autumn of 1965. There were allegations of French government complicity.

desk, which drawer." He told me the name. I told D. D. told the movement. We were so much in the habit of punishing, fighting, getting rid of people, and above all of "not having enough time," that we decided to kill the person concerned at the Liberation. We even chose the place, an open space at Verrières. But when the Liberation came we unanimously dropped the whole thing.

Rabier suffers because I don't put on weight. He says, "I can't bear it." He can bear to arrest people, to send them to their death, but he can't bear that, he can't bear my not putting on weight when he wants me to. He brings me food. I give it to my concierge or throw it down a drain. Money, no—I tell him I'll never accept money. Superstition still survives on that score.

What he would have liked, apart from the bookshop, was to become an expert on pictures and objets d'art. He said in his application to be made an official appraiser that he'd been "art critic on the paper *Les Débats*, curator of the château at Roquebrune, and consultant to the P.L.M. Company. And now," he wrote, "having acquired wide experience in documentation and analysis, and being passionately devoted to all matters concerning the arts, both ancient and modern, I consider myself qualified to carry out any duties entrusted to me, however weighty or difficult."

He also makes appointments with me in the rue Jacob, the rue des Saints-Pères. And in the rue Lecourbe.

Every time I'm going to see Rabier—and this is to go on right to the end—I act as if I were going to be killed. As if he knew all about my activities. Every time, every day.

They were arrested, taken, sent far away from France. And then never the slightest news of them, never the least sign of life, nothing. People weren't even told there was no point in waiting any more, that they were dead. The others didn't even put an end to hope, they let the pain go on for years. The same with the political deportees. In their case too there was no point in telling people. They don't say there's no point in waiting for them any more, they'll never be seen again, ever. But when you think about it, you suddenly ask yourself who else did that. Who? Who?

This time it's in the rue de Sèvres. We come from the direction of the Duroc metro, go past the rue Dupin, where my husband and sister-in-law were arrested. It's five o'clock in the afternoon. It's July already. Rabier stops. He's holding his bicycle in his right hand, his left is on my shoulder, his face is turned toward the rue Dupin. "Look," he says. "Today it's exactly four weeks to the day since we met."

I don't answer. I think, "It's all over."

"One day," Rabier goes on, with a broad smile, "one day I had to arrest a German deserter. First I had to get to know him, and then I had to follow him wherever he went. For a fortnight I saw him every day, for hours and hours every day. We became friends. He was a remarkable man. After four weeks I led him to a doorway where two of my colleagues were waiting to arrest him. He was shot forty-eight hours later."

He added, "That day, too, we'd known each other for four weeks."

His hand was still on my shoulder. The summer of the Liberation had turned to ice.

In my fear the blood ebbs from my head, the mechanism of vision wavers. I can see the tall buildings at the Sèvres crossing swaying about in the sky and the sidewalks going hollow and black. I can't hear properly. But the deafness is relative. The street noises are muffled, like the regular murmur of the sea. But I can hear Rabier's voice quite clearly. I just have time to think that this is the last time I shall ever see a street. But I can't tell which street it is. I ask Rabier, "Why do you tell me this?"

"Because I'm going to ask you to come with me," says Rabier.

I realized I'd always been expecting it. I'd been told that as soon as terror is confirmed, relief follows, peace. It's true. There on the sidewalk I was already arrested, inaccessible to, escaping from, the very creator of fear: Rabier himself. Rabier speaks again: "But I shall ask *you* to come with me to a restaurant where you've never been before. It will give me great pleasure to ask you to be my guest."

He has started to walk on. Before the first and second sentences there's been time to go a certain distance, a bit less than a minute and a half, long enough to get to the square Boucicaut. He stops again, and this time he looks at me. Through a fog I see him laugh. In a most cruel and terrible countenance, a burst of indecent laughter. Vulgarity spreads over it, too, nauseating. This is a trick he must play on the women he mixes with, prostitutes no doubt. After he's played his trick, they owe him their lives. I think this must be exactly how he managed to have women every so often during the year he was at the rue des Saussaies.

Rabier was afraid of his German colleagues. Germans were afraid of Germans. Rabier didn't realize how much the Germans frightened the people of countries occupied by their armies. The Germans were frightening in the same way as the Huns, in the same way as wolves, criminals, and above all, psychotic criminals. I've never discovered how to express it, how to tell those who didn't live through it what sort of fear it was.

I learned during his trial that Rabier used a false identity, that he'd taken the name from a cousin who'd died somewhere near Nice. That he was a German.

Rabier leaves me that evening at Sèvres-Babylone, beaming, pleased with himself.

I hadn't yet sentenced him to death.

I walk home. I can remember quite clearly the rue de Sèvres, a slight curve before the rue des Saints-Pères, and the rue du Dragon. You can walk in the street, there are no cars.

Suddenly freedom is bitter. I've just come to know the total loss of hope and the emptiness that follows; you don't remember, it creates no memory. I think I feel a slight regret at having failed to die while still living. But I go on walking, I move from the street to the sidewalk, then back into the street. I walk, my feet walk.

I can't remember what restaurant it is—it was a black market restaurant, patronized by collaborators, members of the Militia, the Gestapo. It wasn't yet the restaurant in the rue Saint-Georges. He thinks that by inviting me out to eat he's keeping me comparatively healthy. In that way he saves me from despair; in his own eyes he's my good angel. What man would have resisted this role? He doesn't. These lunches are the worst part of the memory—restaurants with closed doors and "friends" knocking on them, butter on the tables, fresh cream overflowing in every dish, juicy meat, wine. I'm not hungry. He is in despair.

One day he arranges to meet me at the Café de Flore. As usual he's not there when I arrive, either on the boulevard or in the café. I sit at the second table on the left as you go in. I haven't known Rabier long. He doesn't know exactly where I live, but he knows it's somewhere in the Saint-Germain-des-Prés area. That's why he's chosen to meet me that day in the Flore. The fashionable café, the café of the existentialists.

But in a few days I've become as careful as he is; I've become his policeman, the one through whom he'll die. Fear, as it grows, corroborates the certainty: he is in my hands.

I'd had time to give warning. Two friends are walking up and down outside the Flore to warn everyone not to approach me. So I'm comparatively calm. I'm starting to get used to the fear of dying. That sounds impossible. Perhaps I should say I was starting to get used to the idea of dying.

What he does at the Flore he will never do again. He puts his briefcase on the table. He opens it. He takes out a revolver. He does all this without a word of explanation. Then from between his leather belt and his trouser pocket he produces a watch chain that looks as if it's made of gold. He says to me, "Look, it's the chain for the handcuffs—it's gold. The key is gold too."

He opens the briefcase again and takes out the pair of handcuffs, lays them down beside the revolver. All this in the Flore. This is a great day for him, being seen there with all the trappings of the perfect policeman. I don't know what he's after. Does he want to make me risk the greatest possible shame, that of being seen at the same table as an agent of the Gestapo, or does he merely want to convince me that he's really that and nothing else, the one whose mission it is to inflict death on whatever is not Nazi? He gets a pack of photographs out of his briefcase, selects one of them, and puts it down in front of me.

"Look at this photo," he says.

I look. It's Morland. The photo's very large, almost life-size. François Morland looks back at me, straight in the eye, smiling. I say, "I don't recognize it. Who is it?"

I didn't expect it at all. Beside the photo, Rabier's hands. Shaking. Rabier is trembling with hope because he thinks I'm going to recognize François Morland. He says, "Morland . . ." He waits. "Doesn't the name mean anything to you?"

"Morland . . ."

"François Morland—he's the head of the movement your husband belonged to."

I'm still looking at the photographs. I ask, "In that case I should know him?"

"Not necessarily."

"Do you have any other photographs?

He has one.

I note the light gray suit, the very short hair, the bow tie, the mustache.

"If you tell me how I can find this man, your husband will be set free during the night—he'll be back home tomorrow morning."

Too light a gray, worst of all the mustache, hair too short. Double-breasted suit. Bow tie too noticeable.

Rabier is not smiling at all now; he's still trembling. I'm not trembling. When it's not just your life that's involved, you find what you need to say. I find what I must say and do. I am saved. I say, "Even if I knew him it would be disgusting of me to tell you what you ask. I don't know how you dare to ask me."

While I'm saying this I look at the other photo.

He sounds less sure: "This man's worth two hundred and fifty thousand francs. But that's not the reason. It's very important to me."

Morland's fate is in my hands. I'm afraid for him. I'm no longer afraid for myself. Morland has become my child. My child is threatened, I risk my life to defend him. I am responsible for him. Suddenly it's Morland who's risking his life. Rabier goes on:

"I tell you, I swear—your husband would leave Fresnes this very night."

"Even if I knew him I wouldn't tell you."

At last I looked at the people in the café. No one seemed to have seen the handcuffs and the revolver on the table.

"But you don't know him?"

"That's right—it so happens I don't know him."

Rabier puts the photographs back in the briefcase. He's still trembling a bit, he isn't smiling. Just a touch of sadness in his expression, but very brief and quickly banished.

I also write down the latest news to make him laugh, to make Robert L. laugh. He laughs, roars with laughter. I write about the gold chain, the gold key to the handcuffs. I can hear Robert L. burst out laughing.

Rabier had carried out twenty-four arrests during the period before we met, but he'd have liked to have a lot more warrants. He'd have liked to arrest four times as many people, especially important ones. He saw his job as a policeman as a chance to make good. Up till then he'd arrested Jews, parachutists, third-rate members of the Resistance. The arrest of François Morland would have been an event of unprecedented importance in his life. I'm sure he saw a possible link between Morland's arrest and the art bookshop. According to his rambling notions, such a distinguished arrest might have brought the person responsible quite a reward. Rabier never allowed for the German defeat. If he could imagine being a policeman one day and the manager of an art bookshop in Paris the next, his dream could only come true through a German victory. Only a Franco-German Nazi society ruling over France could appreciate his services and nourish him in its bosom.

One day Rabier told me that if the Germans were forced to leave Paris—an eventuality he didn't believe in for a moment—he'd stay on in France on a secret mission. I think it was in a restaurant that he said it, between courses, offhand.

With what money I have left I buy three kilos of weevilly beans and a kilo of butter, which has gone up again and costs twelve thousand francs a kilo. I spend all that money to keep myself alive.

We see each other every day, D. and I. We talk about Rabier. I tell D. what he has said. I find it very hard to convey his fundamental stupidity. He's enveloped in it, there's no getting through it. Everything about him derives from it—feelings, imagination, and the worst kind of optimism. You see it at once. I've probably never met anyone so lonely as this purveyor of dead men.

In group photographs of the Central Committee of the Supreme Soviet in Moscow, the murderer-members look to me as if they're lonely in the same way as Rabier—the solitude of cholera victims, or worse, with moth-eaten souls, each loneliness in its own disguise, its teeth chattering for fear of its neighbor, for fear of tomorrow's execution.

. . .

But there was something about Rabier that made him even lonelier than the rest. Apart from the art book-shop, he must have been waiting for a nightmare to end. But that was something he never mentioned to me. For him to have assumed the identity of a dead man, to have stolen the identity of that young man who died near Nice, there must have been some criminal act in Rabier's former life, an unresolved episode still action-able under the law. He was living under an assumed name. A French name. And that makes a man even lonelier than other men. I was the only person who listened to Rabier. But Rabier himself wasn't audible. I'm speaking of his voice, Rabier's voice. It was made up, calculated, an artificial organ. Detoned, you could call it; but what was wrong with it was something much more, something more shocking. It was partly because it wasn't audible, listenable-to, that I listened to it so intently. Every so often it would have a trace of accent. But what accent? At the most you might have said, "Is it a trace of a German accent?" It was that which prevented him from having any kind of identity, that strangeness, seeping out from the memory into the voice. No one ever spoke like that who had a childhood and schoolfriends in the country of their birth.

Rabier didn't know anyone. He didn't even talk to his colleagues, I got the impression they didn't want him to. He could only talk to those whose lives were in his power, those he sent to the ovens or the concentra-tion camps, or those left behind longing for news, their wives.

If he'd reprieved the German deserter for three weeks, it was to have someone to talk to for three weeks, to talk to about himself, Rabier. I'd been his mistake. He could have arrested me whenever he liked. But in me he'd found an audience he'd probably never had before; one that never wearied. It confused him so much to be listened to like that that he got careless, making slips that were harmless at first and then became more and more serious, but that were in any case to lead him quite inevitably to his own execution.

I wake up in the night, in the night the void of absence is vast, shot through with terrible fear. Then I remember that no one has any news yet. It's later, when the news starts to arrive, that the waiting begins.

Rabier is married to a young woman of twenty-six. He's forty-one. He's got a child who must be between four and five. He lives with his family in the inner suburbs of Paris. He rides in on his bicycle every day. I don't think I ever heard what he told his wife about what he did. She didn't know he belonged to the Gestapo. He's tall, fair, shortsighted—he wears gold-rimmed spectacles. He has laughing blue eyes, hinting at his body's bursting health. He's very well groomed. Every day he wears a clean shirt. Every day his shoes are polished. His fingernails are immaculate. He's clean with an unforgettable, meticulous, almost maniacal cleanliness. He must regard it as a matter of principle. He dresses like a gentleman. In that job you need to look like a gentleman. He beats people up, fights, works with guns, blood, and tears—and he looks as if he works with white gloves on. He has the hands of a surgeon.

All through the early days of the German collapse, Rabier smiles and says, "Rommel will counterattack. I have information to that effect."

We've just come out of a *café-tabac* near the Bourse and are walking along the street. It's a fine day. We talk about the war. You had to talk all the time so as not to seem sad. So I talk, I say the Normandy front hasn't advanced for weeks. That Paris is hungry. That a kilo of butter costs thirteen thousand francs. He says, "Germany is invincible."

We go on walking. He looks closely at everything around him, the empty streets, the crowd on the sidewalks. The communiqués make it quite clear, their front is going to crumble any day now, the whole world is waiting for it, waiting for the first withdrawal. He looks at Paris with love; he knows it very well. In streets like these he has arrested people. Every street has its memories, its shrieks, its shouts, its sobs. These memories don't cause Rabier any pain. He and his like are the gardeners of that garden, Paris, of the streets they adore and that are now free of Jews. He remembers only his good deeds, he has no recollection of having acted harshly. When he speaks of the people he's arrested he becomes quite moved: they all understood the sad necessity he was under to do it, they never made any difficulties, they were all charming.

"You're sad—I can't bear it when you're sad."

"I'm not sad."

"Yes, you are—you don't say anything."

"I want to see my husband."

"I know someone at Fresnes who may have news of him, who'll tell you what train he'll be on. But she'll want money."

I say I don't have any money, but I do have some jewelry, a gold ring with a very fine topaz. He says we can always try. The next day I bring him the ring. The day after that he tells me he's passed the ring to the person in question. Then he doesn't mention it again. Several days go by. I ask him about the ring. He says he's tried to see the person in question but hasn't been able to, he thinks she can't be working at Fresnes any more, she must have gone back to Germany. I don't ask whether she took the ring with her.

I've always believed that Rabier never passed that ring on, that he took it himself, that he invented the story about the woman at Fresnes just to keep me hanging on, to make me believe my husband was still there and that he, Rabier, could still try to get in touch with him. He couldn't give me back my ring without revealing that he'd been lying.

He always has that smart briefcase with him. It's unusually elegant, and I've always thought it was a bit of loot he'd picked up while making an arrest or searching an empty apartment. He never had anything in it except the handcuffs and the revolver. Never any papers. Except the photographs of Morland, that time in the Flore.

He also carries with him, in the inside pockets of his jacket, two other revolvers of lesser caliber than the one in the briefcase. According to the lawyer who defended him, F., he sometimes carried yet another two revolvers, also in inside pockets especially made in his jacket.

This immoderate carrying of revolvers is urged in Rabier's favor at his trial.

"Look at the idiot, carrying six revolvers on him at once!" says F., his lawyer.

Rabier is alone in the dock. He listens intently. Everything that's said concerns him. He doesn't deny the six revolvers. He's being talked about, so he's achieved what he wanted most in life. People are talking about him, people are questioning him, and he is answering. He doesn't understand himself why he carries six revolvers and a pair of gold handcuffs and a gold chain and key. And no one explains it to him.

He is alone in the dock. He isn't anxious, he seems supernaturally brave, so indifferent does he appear to the death that awaits him. The looks he gives us are friendly. D. and I are the only ones who don't say much, not as much as the others. Rabier will say, "They've been fair enemies."

I go to Fresnes. More and more of us go to Fresnes every morning to try to get some news. We wait outside the monumental gate of the prison. We question everyone who comes out, German soldiers as well as French cleaning women. The answer is always the same: "I don't know. We don't know anything."

Sometimes, beside the railroad tracks on which trains carrying Jews and deportees used to go, people find scraps of papers with names on them, the address to which they're to be sent, and the number of the train. Many of these bits of paper reach the person they're addressed to. Sometimes there's another note attached to the first, saying where, in France, Germany, or Silesia, the first piece of paper was found. We begin to wait for that too, for those notes thrown out of the trucks. Just in case.

The German defense of Normandy collapses. We try to find out what they're going to do with their prisoners: if they're going to speed up the deportation of political detainees to Germany, or shoot them before they themselves leave. For several days buses have been coming out of the prison full of men under armed guard. Sometimes they shout out bits of information. One morning, on the platform at the back of one of the buses, I see Robert L. I run after the bus and ask where they're going. Robert L. shouts something. I think I hear him say "Compiègne." I fall down in a faint. People come up to me and confirm that I did hear "Compiègne." Compiègne is the marshaling yard from which trains are directed to the camps. His sister must have gone already. I think he's not so likely to be shot now, since there are still trains. I was to learn later —probably from Morland, I can't quite remember— that I was wrong and that Robert L. was sent to Germany on April 28, in the train carrying serious cases.

It was that same evening that I told D. of my decision to hand Rabier over to the movement so that they could move fast, before he had time to escape.

· · ·

The first thing to do is have some members of the movement identify Rabier. Suddenly there isn't much time. I'm afraid of dying. Everyone's afraid of dying. It's a terrible fear. We don't know the Germans, but we're sure they are murderers. I know Rabier may kill me, in the same way as a child might know it. It's confirmed every day. Already, though he phones me every day, there are often several days running when, as he puts it, he's "not able to see me." I suppose they must be removing the files. Then one day he can see me again. He asks if I can have lunch with him. I say yes. As usual, he calls again half an hour later to tell me the time and the place. D. calls me back as arranged. He says that to be on the safe side two of them will come to identify him.

It's a restaurant in the rue Saint-Georges, near the Gare Saint-Lazare, patronized almost exclusively by agents of the Gestapo. The news being what it is, Rabier is probably afraid to go where he's not among colleagues.

He's waiting for me, as usual, not in the restaurant but at the intersection of the rue Saint-Georges and the rue Notre-Dame-de-Lorette.

The place is full. It's rather dark, divided into two sections both the same size, with one looking out on the street. The sections are separated by a long bench covered with artificial leather. Rabier and I sit at the table right at the back of the section overlooking the street.

I don't look up until I'm sitting beside him. My colleagues aren't here yet. The restaurant is almost full.

Nearly all the customers have briefcases under their arms. Rabier greets everyone, but they scarcely bother to reply. This confirms my opinion that even here, among his own people, he's alone.

I lower my eyes again. The lids are like lead. They shelter me from other people's scrutiny. I'm frightened and I'm ashamed. I try to reduce the situation to its lowest terms: I'm the only one here not employed by the German police. I'm afraid of being killed, ashamed of being alive. I can't think clearly any more. What makes me grow a bit thinner every day is shame, as well as fear and hunger. My fear for Robert L. is confined to fear about the war. We don't know yet about the camps. It's August 1944. It's only in the spring that we'll find out. Germany is losing the territories it conquered, but its own soil is still intact. Nothing has yet been discovered about Nazi atrocities. What we're afraid of for the prisoners and for the deportees is the fantastic debacle that is imminent. We're still innocent of all knowledge of what has been happening in Germany since 1933. We're still living in the first age of humanity, pure, virginal, for another few months. Nothing has been revealed about the Human Race. I am a prey to elementary emotions that are perfectly clear. I'm ashamed of sitting here beside Pierre Rabier of the Gestapo, but I'm also ashamed of having to lie to this member of the Gestapo, this hunter of Jews. The shame extends even to the shame of perhaps having to die at his hands.

. . .

The news is bad for them. Montgomery broke through at Arromanches during the night. The GHQ in Normandy have sent for Rommel to come at once.

At the next table there's a couple whom Rabier apparently knows slightly. They all start talking about the war. I lower my eyes again or look out into the street. I feel it's impossible for me to look at them without incurring great danger. I suddenly believe that here people can see through other people's eyes, their glances, their smiles, their table manners, no matter how natural they try to seem. The woman at the next table says, addressing Rabier and me, "They've already come, you know, during the night. They banged at the door. We didn't ask who it was, and we didn't turn on the light."

I realize that members of the Resistance went to their place last night. And that the door of their apartment was reinforced and the others couldn't get in. Rabier smiles, turns to me, and says quietly, "*She*'s afraid."

He orders some wine. The others still haven't come. The wine alters everything. The fear melts away. I ask him, "And what about your door?"

"It's not reinforced. I'm not afraid, as you know."

For the first time I talk to him about the woman who had fainted and whom he was carrying along in the corridors of the Gestapo when I met him for the second time. I say I know she'd been subjected to the bathtub torture. He laughs as at the naiveté of a child. He says it's nothing, really nothing, just a bit unpleasant, there's been a lot of exaggeration about it. I look at him. He's less important already. He's nothing. He's nobody, just an agent of the German police. I suddenly see him as an extra in a farcical tragedy as idiotic as a bad rhetorical exercise, already stricken by a death of the same stamp, a death that is itself devalued, not genuine, deflated. D. has told me they'll try to kill him in the next few days. The place has already been chosen. They have to be quick, before he leaves Paris.

It's impossible to imagine D. arriving in this restaurant. I believe that as soon as they come in, so handsome, so young, the German police will recognize them. And I believe they'll behave foolishly. The kind of fear I've been living in for weeks with Rabier, the fear of not being able to face up to fear—safety lies in that way of putting it—they don't know this fear. They are innocents. Beside Rabier and me they are innocents, they haven't dabbled in death.

I say to Rabier, "The news isn't good for you."

He helps me to wine, again and again. Never before has he done that, never before have I drunk like this. As soon as the wine is poured out I swig it down. I say, "The news is good for me."

I laugh. It's the wine. Clearly, it's the wine. Already I can't drink any more of it. He looks at me. He must have died with that look. Already he's distancing himself from us, he's got a halo, already he's what he will be in the dock, already it can't be otherwise: he's a hero.

"One day," says Pierre Rabier, "I had to arrest some Jews. We went into their apartment and there was nobody there. On the dining-room table there were some colored crayons and a child's drawing. I went away again without waiting for the parents." He even told me that if he'd known about it he'd have warned me about my own arrest. I translate this to mean if someone other than himself had had to arrest me. That's how he is—absolutely indifferent to human suffering in general, but indulging himself in the luxury of his own forms of squeamishness. And to this we owe our lives, the little Jew and I.

I look at him again. With the wine, I do so more and more often. He talks about Germany. I can't share his faith. According to him Germany is a mystery, especially to other people, including the defeated French.

"But it's all over—finished," I say. "In three days Montgomery will be in Paris."

"You don't understand. It's impossible. Our strength is inexhaustible. Only Germans can understand."

He's going to die of divine retribution. That's what the papers will say. I say he's going to die before three nights are out. I remember perfectly: I looked at his new shirt. He was wearing his brown suit. His open-necked shirt was light fawn to match his suit. I thought it was a pity for the new shirt to be on a condemned man. And I also thought, very intently, looking at him very intently, "Don't buy any shoes this afternoon, because it isn't worth it." He doesn't hear. I think he's barred from hearing thoughts, barred from everything, all there is for him to do is die.

I think that if he's making me drink like this it's because he's already in despair over the defeat. It's strange he doesn't realize it. He thinks he's making me drink to try to make me go to a hotel with him. But he doesn't know yet what he's going to do with me in the hotel, whether he's going to possess me or kill me. He says, "Oh, how awful—you've lost weight again. I can't bear it."

That morning I have a very clear impression that it's the man who arrests Jews and sends them to the gas chambers who can't stand the sight I present to him, that of a woman who's thin and ill—because he's the cause of it. He was often to say that if he'd known, he wouldn't have arrested my husband. Every day he decided my fate, and every day if he'd known, he said, my fate would have been different. Whether he knew or not, before or after, my fate was in his hands. It's a power that's bestowed on the police. But usually its members are cut off from their victims, whereas he, knowing me, saw his power confirmed, and had the marvelous good luck of being able to enter into the darkness of his own acts, to enjoy the clandestinity that hid him from himself.

I suddenly notice that the atmosphere in the restaurant is one of great fear. It was when my own fear faded that I saw the other one. The forty or fifty people there were all threatened with death in the next few days. A massacre.

I can remember the wine. It was cool. Red. I remember he didn't drink any himself.

"You don't know Germany, or Hitler. Hitler's a military genius. I have it on reliable authority that within two days enormous reinforcements will be coming from Germany. They must already have crossed the frontier. The English advance will be halted."

"I don't believe it. Hitler isn't a military genius."

I add, "I have information too. You'll see."

The woman nods in my direction and asks, "What's she saying?"

Rabier turns toward her. Suddenly he's cold, distant.

"She doesn't share our point of view about the war," says Rabier.

The woman doesn't understand what he's saying or why he's so curt all of a sudden.

I see them parking their bikes out in the street. It's D. For the second person they've chosen a girl. I look down. Rabier looks at them and then looks away again, he hasn't noticed anything. She must be about eighteen. She's a friend. I could watch them go through a furnace more easily than this. They go through the restaurant, looking for a table. There aren't many empty. They must be starting to be afraid they won't find one. I see them without looking at them. I drink. There, they've got a table. It's facing ours, two tables away. I notice there was another a bit farther away which they didn't take, so they must have chosen the nearest there was. Perhaps they've already identified with the parts they have to play; they're full of the recklessness and impetuosity of children. I scan their faces, I see the joy in their eyes. They see it in mine.

Rabier speaks: "Yesterday I arrested a young man of twenty over near the Invalides. His mother was there.

It was terrible. We arrested the young man before his mother's very eyes."

A waiter has gone up to their table. They're reading the menu. I eat something, I don't know what it is. Rabier goes on: "It was terrible. The woman was shrieking. She said he was a good boy, she was his mother, she knew, we must believe her. But he, the boy, didn't say anything."

A violinist has come into the restaurant. That'll make it easier. I reply:

"And the boy didn't say anything?"

"Not a word. It was extraordinary. He was completely calm. He tried to comfort his mother before he came away with us. Oh, he was so much closer to us than to his mother, it was extraordinary."

They call the violinist over. I wait, I don't answer Rabier. There—it's a tune I know, we used to sing it when we met. I start to laugh uncontrollably and can't stop. Rabier looks at me, puzzled.

"What's the matter?"

"It's the end of the war. This is it, it's the end, the end of Germany. I'm laughing with glee."

He still smiles at me kindly and says something unforgettable. Charming too—if one is a Nazi.

"I can understand that that's what you hope. I do understand, really. But it isn't possible."

"Germany has lost, it's all over."

I laugh, I can't stop. They're laughing, too, over at their table. The violinist is sawing away like mad. Rabier says, "You're cheerful—I'm pleased about that, anyway."

I say, "You could have left that young man alone. What difference could it make to you, the last day before the end? You killed him to prove to yourself that the war wasn't over, didn't you?"

We knew that already, D. and I.

"No. The war won't stop for people like me. I'll go on serving Germany till I die. I won't be leaving France, if you want to know."

"You won't be able to stay."

I've never spoken like this before. I more or less tell him who I am. And he doesn't listen.

"Germany can't lose, you know that really. In a couple of days you'll get a surprise."

"No. It's over. In a couple of days, or three, or four, Paris will be free."

The woman at the next table can hear all we're saying in spite of the violin. My fear has gone. Probably because of the wine. The woman shouts, "But what does she mean?"

"We arrested her husband," says Rabier.

"Oh, so that's it . . ."

"That's it," says Rabier. "She's French."

Lots of the people here are looking at my friends, this pair of sweethearts who've suddenly appeared in their midst. They're apparently not curious about who they are. They smile, they're reassured: death isn't so close after all.

The violinist plays the song again for the two stray lovers. I realize that they and I are the only ones who are not afraid. The songs the violinist plays are recent, songs of the German Occupation. For them they're already poignant, over. Already in the past. I ask Rabier, "Do reinforced doors really work?"

"They're expensive"—he's still smiling—"but they work."

The woman from the Gestapo is looking at me fascinated; she'd like to find out something about the end. I come from what is a far country for her, I come from France. I believe she'd like to ask me if it really is the end.

"What are you going to do?" I ask.

"I've thought about having a little bookshop," says Rabier. "I've always been a bibliophile. Perhaps you might help me."

I try to look him in the face, but can't. I say, "Who knows?"

I suddenly remember something I've been told about fear. That amid a hail of machine gun fire you notice the existence of your skin. A sixth sense emerges. I'm drunk. It wouldn't take much to make me tell him he's going to be killed. Perhaps one glass of wine would do it. Suddenly I'm full of the sort of ease and well-being you feel when you dive into the sea in summer. Everything seems possible. So as not to deceive him, him, the informer. Tell him, tell him he's going to be killed. In a street in the sixth arrondissement. Perhaps it's only the thought of what D. would say that keeps me from telling him.

We've left the restaurant.

We're both on bicycles. He's a few yards in front of me. I remember how he pedaled. Calmly. A Paris racer.

He has iron fetters around his ankles, which makes me laugh. His briefcase is on the carrier, tied on tight with a strap.

I raise my right hand for a moment and pretend to aim at him—bang!

He pedals on into eternity. He doesn't turn around. I laugh. I aim at the back of his neck. We're going very fast. His back stretches out, very big, ten feet away from me. Impossible to miss it, it's so big—bang! I laugh and clutch at the handlebars so as not to fall off. My aim's good. The middle of the back strikes me as safer. Bang!

He stops. I stop behind him. Then I come up level with him. He's pale. He's trembling. At last. He says in a whisper, "Come with me, I have a friend who's got a studio near here. We could have a drink together."

It was a big intersection, the one at Châteaudun, I think. There were lots of people and we were lost in the crowd on the sidewalk.

"Just for a minute," begs Rabier. "Come just for a minute."

I say, "No. Some other time."

He knew I'd never go. He'd asked just for the sake of asking, as if before saying goodbye. He was very worked up, but not really serious. He was already too full of fear. And perhaps despair.

He suddenly gives up. Goes in through an archway and walks away with his civil servant's gait.

He never phoned me again.

• • •

At eleven o'clock one night a few days later there came the Liberation of Paris. He too must have heard the enormous din of all the church bells in Paris and perhaps seen the whole population out in the streets. That inexpressible happiness. And then he probably went and hid in his lair in the rue des Renaudes. His wife and son had already left for the provinces and he was alone. His wife, summoned to appear at the trial—insignificant but good-looking, said a witness—said she didn't know anything about his police activities.

We tried to extract him from the due process of law and kill him ourselves, to save him from going through the usual channels of the courts. We'd even chosen the place—in the boulevard Saint-Germain, I can't remember exactly where. But we couldn't find him. So we told the police about him. They found him. He was in the camp at Drancy, alone.

I gave evidence twice at the trial. The second time because I'd forgotten before to mention the little Jewish child that he spared. I asked to be heard again. I said I'd forgotten to say he had saved a Jewish family, and told the story of the child's drawing. I also said I'd heard since then that he had saved two Jewish women, whom he smuggled into unoccupied France. The judge yelled at me, "Make up your mind—first you accused him, now you defend him. We haven't got time to waste here!" I answered that I wanted to tell the truth, wanted it to be said, in case those two facts might get him off the death penalty. The judge asked me to leave; he was furious. The whole courtroom was against me. I left.

I learned at Rabier's trial that he'd put his savings into buying first editions. First editions of Mallarmé, Gide, Lamartine, and Chateaubriand, and perhaps of Giraudoux too: books he'd never read and never would read, that perhaps he tried to read and couldn't. For me this is typical of the Rabier I knew, just as much as his job was. This, added to his gentlemanly manner, his faith in Nazi Germany, his cheap kindnesses, his forgetfulness, his rashness, and perhaps also his attachment to me. Me through whom he was to die.

And then Rabier went completely out of my head. I forgot him.

He must have been shot during the winter of 1944–1945. I don't know where. I was told it was probably in the yard of the prison at Fresnes, as usual.

With summer came the German defeat. It was total. It extended all over Europe. The summer came with its dead, its survivors, and with the unthinkable suffering reverberating from the German concentration camps.

ALBERT OF THE CAPITALS
TER OF THE MILITIA

These texts ought to have come straight after the diary transcribed in The War, *but I decided to leave a space in which the din of war might die down.*

Thérèse is me. The person who tortures the informer is me. So also is the one who feels like making love to Ter, the member of the Militia. Me. I give you the torturer along with the rest of the texts. Learn to read them properly: they are sacred.

ALBERT OF THE CAPITALS

It was two days since the first jeep, since the capture of the Kommandantur in the place de l'Opéra. It was Sunday.

At five in the afternoon the waiter from a bistro near the building where the Richelieu group used to meet came running in. "There's a fellow in my place who used to work with the German police. He's from Noisy. I come from there, too. Everyone there knows about him. You could still catch him. But you'll have to hurry."

D. chose three people for the job. The news spread.

For years we'd heard about them, at first we imagined we saw them everywhere. This one might be the first we could be sure about. Now we had time to make sure. And to see what an informer was like. We were extremely curious. Already we were more curious about what we'd lived through unknowingly under the Occupation than about the strange experiences we'd been living through in the last week, since the Liberation.

The men that made up the group swarmed into the hall, the bar, the entrance. For two days they hadn't been fighting any more; there was nothing more for the group to do. Nothing but eat and sleep and start to squabble over guns and cars and girls. Some drove off every morning in hopes of still finding a fight somewhere, going farther away every day and coming back at night.

He arrived, escorted by the three comrades who'd been sent to fetch him.

He was brought into the "bar." That was what we called a sort of cloakroom with a counter, from which food had been distributed during the insurrection. He stood for an hour in the middle of the bar. D. examined his papers. The men looked at him. Came up to him. Stared. Insulted him. "Bastard. Scum. Traitor."

Fifty years old. Squints a bit. Wears glasses. A stiff collar and a tie. He's fat, short, ill-shaven. His hair is gray. He smiles all the time, as if it were all a joke.

In his pockets he has an identity card; a photograph of an old woman, his wife; a photograph of himself; eight hundred francs; an address book with mostly incomplete addresses, just Christian names, surnames, and phone numbers. D. notices one strange entry which becomes more and more familiar as he looks through the book. He shows it to Thérèse. Every so often in the early pages it occurs in full: "Albert of the Capitals." Later it becomes just "Albert" or "Capitals." In the last pages, just "Cap" or "Al."

"What does it mean—Albert of the Capitals?" asks D.

The informer looks at him. He looks as if he's trying to think. Like someone sincerely sorry he can't remember, who'd like to be able to remember, who's sincerely trying to.

"Albert of the what?" asks the informer.

"Albert of the Capitals."

"Albert of the Capitals?"

"Yes, Albert of the Capitals," says D.

D. has put the address book down on the counter. He comes over to the informer empty-handed. He looks him steadily in the eye. Thérèse picks up the address book and flicks through it. It occurs for the last time on August 11: "Al." Today is the twenty-seventh. She puts the address book down again, and now she too looks at the informer. All the others have fallen silent. D. is standing, facing the informer.

"You don't remember?" he asks.

He moves a bit nearer.

The informer draws back. His eyes flicker.

"Oh yes!" says the informer. "How stupid of me! It's Albert, the waiter at the Capitals, a café near the Gare de l'Est. I live at Noisy-le-Sec, so of course I sometimes have a drink at the Capitals when I get off the train . . ."

D. comes back to the counter. He sends someone to fetch the waiter from the bistro. The man comes back. The waiter's already gone home. Everyone in the bistro knows about it. But he hasn't told them any details.

"What's he like, this Albert?" D. asks the informer.

"Short. Fair. A very nice fellow," says the informer, smiling, conciliatory.

D. turns to the comrades standing at the entrance to the bar.

"Take the Peugeot and go right away," he says.

The informer looks at D. He stops smiling. At first he looks dazed, then he pulls himself together.

"No, monsieur, you're making a mistake . . . You're wrong, monsieur."

In the background: "Swine. Traitor. You'll soon be

laughing on the other side of your face. You've got it coming to you. Scum."

D. goes on searching him. A half-empty pack of Gauloises, a pencil stub, a new automatic pencil. A key.

Three men have left. You can hear the Peugeot starting up.

"You're making a mistake, monsieur."

D. goes on searching. The informer is sweating. He seems not to want to talk to anyone but D., probably because D.'s manner is polite and he doesn't insult him. He speaks correct and careful French. The informer is obviously trying to put himself on the same side as D., to distance himself from the other members of the group, to establish a sort of complicity, a sort of fraternity with someone of his own class.

"You've got the wrong man. I'm not laughing, monsieur, believe me; I don't feel at all like laughing."

There's nothing left in his pockets now. All there was is on the counter.

"Put him in the room next to the cashier's office."

Two members of the group come over to the informer. He gives D. a look of entreaty: "Monsieur, it's the truth, *please* . . ."

D. sits down, picks up the address book, and looks at it.

"Come on," says one of the men, "and don't try to get smart."

The informer goes out with the two men. Another member of the group whistles a cheerful tune on the other side of the room. Most of the men go out of the bar and stand around the entrance, waiting for the car to come back. D. and Thérèse are alone in the bar.

Every so often there's a burst of machine gun fire in the distance. We've got used to placing them: that one's from over near the Bibliothèque Nationale, from the corner of the boulevard des Italiens. The men talk about informers and their fate. When they hear the sound of a car approaching they stop talking and go out. No, it's not the Peugeot. One of them whistles, the same tune again, cheerful, lively.

A faint rumble of sound can be heard from the boulevard des Italiens, a continuous roar of engines, cheers, singing, women shouting, men shouting, all mixed and mingled and dense. For two days and nights, one vast ooze of honey.

"The main thing," Thérèse says to D., "is to find out if this man really is an informer. We'll only waste time over Albert of the Capitals, then the mothball crowd* will come and we'll have had it, because they won't get anything out of him and they'll let him go. Or else they'll say he might be useful."

D. says we must be patient.

Thérèse says not any more, we've been patient long enough.

D. says we should never be impatient. Now more than ever we must be patient.

He says that starting with Albert of the Capitals we might be able to trace the whole chain back, link by link. He says the informer is unimportant, a nobody,

---

* In French, *naphtalinés*, "mothballed ones": Members of the army who had withdrawn early from the struggle against Germany and put their uniforms away, so that when they emerged to take part in the Liberation their uniforms were new-looking and smelled of mothballs.

paid by piecework, so much a head. That those we need to get are the higher-ups, the ones who sat in offices and signed the death warrants of hundreds of Jews and members of the Resistance. And were paid fifty thousand francs a month for it. Those were the ones we needed to get, according to D.

Thérèse listens vaguely. She looks at the time.

One evening, a week ago, Roger, the other leader of the group, came into the canteen and said they'd taken seven Germans prisoner. He described how. He said they'd given them clean straw to sleep on and supplied them with beer. Thérèse got up from the table and shouted abuse at Roger. She said she wished they'd kill German prisoners. Roger laughed. Everyone laughed. Everyone agreed with Roger: it wasn't right to ill-treat German prisoners, they were soldiers who'd been captured in battle. Thérèse went out of the canteen. Everyone had laughed, but since then they'd all rather steered clear of her. All except D.

It's the first time she's been with D. since the other evening. For once D. isn't doing anything. He's waiting for the car to come back. He stares at the door, waiting for Albert of the Capitals. Thérèse is sitting opposite.

"Do you think I was wrong the other evening?" asks Thérèse.

"When?"

"About the German prisoners."

"Of course you were wrong. The others were wrong, too, to be angry with you."

D. offers Thérèse a cigarette, holding out the pack. "Here . . ."

They light up.

"Do you want to question him yourself?" asks D.

"As you like. I don't give a damn."

"Of course," says D.

The car. The three members of the group get out. Alone. D. goes out.

"Well?"

"Huh! Decamped two weeks ago. On vacation, so they said . . ."

"Hell!"

D. goes into the canteen on the first floor. Thérèse goes in too. The men are just finishing dinner. Thérèse hasn't eaten, neither has D.

The men stop and looked at Thérèse and D. It's certain Thérèse is going to question the informer. No more to be said.

Thérèse stands behind D., rather pale. She looks spiteful, solitary. It's been more obvious ever since the Liberation. Ever since she started going to the center, she hasn't been seen arm-in-arm with anyone. During the insurrection she spared no effort—she wasn't unkind but she wasn't warm. She was absent, solitary. She's waiting for a man who may have been shot. This evening it's particularly evident.

Ten members of the group get up and go over to D. and Thérèse. They've all got good reasons for wanting to deal with the informer, even those who laughed the loudest the other evening. D. chooses two who were in Montluc prison near Lyons and who were beaten up.

No more to be said. No one protests, but no one sits down again. They're waiting.

"I'll have something to eat," says D., "then I'll join you. Do you understand, Thérèse? Above all, Albert of the Capitals' address, or the addresses of those he saw most frequently. We must get the whole network."

Thérèse and the two who were in Montluc, Albert and Lucien, go out of the canteen. The others follow automatically; none of them can bring himself to sit down again. There's no electric light in the building except in the part fed by the engines of the press. But that's too far away and probably being used. They'll need a hurricane lamp from down in the bar. Thérèse goes down with the two who were in Montluc. The others go down too, in a group, still keeping a little way behind. When they've collected the lamp they go up a back stairway that leads to the cashier's office in an empty corridor. That's the place. One of the Montluc men opens the door with the key D. gave him. Thérèse goes in first. The two from Montluc go in behind her and shut them all in. The others are left out in the hall. For the moment they don't try to get in.

Sitting on a chair by the table, the informer. He must have been sitting with his head buried in his arms when he heard the noise of the lock. Now he's sitting up. He half turns to see the people coming in. He blinks, dazzled by the light of the hurricane lamp. Lucien puts it in the middle of the table, shining it toward him, the man.

The room is almost empty. The only furniture is two chairs and a table. Thérèse takes the second chair and sits down on the other side of the table, behind the lamp. The informer remains sitting in the light. The other two men flank him on either side, standing behind him in the shadow.

"Undress, and fast," says Albert. "We haven't got time to waste on *you*."

Albert's still too young not to play tough.

The informer stands up. He looks like someone just waking up. He takes off his jacket. His face is pallid, he's very shortsighted, he must see practically nothing in spite of his glasses. He moves very slowly. Thérèse disagrees with her colleague. They've got plenty of time.

He puts his jacket down on the chair. The two men still stand waiting on either side of him. They're all silent, including the informer, including Thérèse. Whispering can be heard from outside the closed door. He takes his time putting his jacket on the chair, does it with care. Slowly he obeys. He has no choice.

Thérèse wonders if it's really necessary to make him undress. Now that he's there, it's not so urgent. She feels nothing any more, nothing, neither hatred nor impatience. Nothing. The only thing is, it's slow. Time is dead as he undresses.

She doesn't know why she doesn't leave. Though she doesn't leave, the idea does cross her mind. Yet now it's inevitable. You'd need to go a long way back to know why, why it's she, Thérèse, who is going to deal with the informer. D. has given him to her. She has taken him. She's got him. But this rare specimen, she no longer wants him. She wants to sleep. She says to herself, "I'm asleep." He takes off his trousers and puts them down, as carefully as before, on top of his jacket.

His underpants are crumpled and gray. "You have to be somewhere, doing something," thinks Thérèse. "Now I'm here, in this dark room, shut in with Albert and Lucien, the two from Montluc, and this betrayer of Jews and members of the Resistance. I'm at the cinema." Once she was on the embankment by the river, the Seine; it was two o'clock in the afternoon, a day in summer, and someone kissed her and said he loved her. She understood then, she understands still. There's a name for everything: that was the day she decided to live with a man. And today, what is that? What will it be? Soon she'll be in the rue Réaumur at the newspaper office, doing her job. People think these things are out of the ordinary. But they're like everything else. Like everything else, they happen to you. Afterward, they have happened to you. They might happen to anyone.

Sitting with her elbows on the table, Thérèse watches. The others watch too. The elder of the two is Lucien, aged twenty-five. He works in a garage in Levallois. He's not very well liked at the center. He fought well but exaggerated when he told about it. A talker. The other one is Albert, an unskilled printing worker, eighteen years old, brought up in an orphanage, one of the bravest when it comes to a fight. He steals all the guns he can find. He stole D.'s revolver. He's short and small. A kid who didn't have enough to eat, who went to work too young, he was only fourteen in 1940. D. doesn't hold it against him that he stole his revolver, he says it's only natural, people like that are the ones who should be allowed to have the guns. Thérèse looks at Albert. He's a funny kid, really. He was the worst with the Germans, he didn't tell all he did to them. One day last week he set fire to a German tank with a bottle of gasoline in the place du Palais-Royal. The bottle broke on the skull of a German and he was burned alive. The informer's socks have holes in them; one big toe, with a dirty toenail, sticks out. They're the socks of someone who hasn't been home for days and has done a lot of walking. He must have been walking about for days scared as hell, then gone back to the bistro, it's what you're bound to do, go back to the bistro where they know you. And then the others came. And he was done for.

They've even made him take his socks off, just as they were probably made to take theirs off in Montluc. It's a bit silly, thinks Thérèse; these fellows are a bit silly. Silly, but they didn't talk in Montluc, not one word. D. was told this by other members of the group, that's why he chose them this evening. It's ten days, more, ten days and nights now that Thérèse has been living with them, giving them wine, cigarettes, bottles of gasoline. Sometimes, when they were tired, they talked to one another about the fighting, the Germans in the tanks, their families and friends. When they didn't come back the others waited for them, didn't sleep. Last Monday they'd waited for Albert all night.

The informer is taking off his socks. Still—they stick to his feet. It's slow work.

"Get a move on," says Albert finally.

Thérèse hadn't noticed Albert's voice before: it's curt and rather high-pitched. She wonders why she waited for him so long the other night. During the fighting everyone waited for everyone else equally. They avoided partiality. Now they'll start again. Start preferring one person to another.

Now it's his tie he's taking off. That's it, his tie. There only one way of doing it. You put your head on one side and tug at one end without undoing the knot. The informer takes off his tie the same way as everyone else.

The informer has a tie. He still had one three months ago. An hour ago. And cigarettes. And an apéritif at about five in the afternoon. There *are* differences between men. Thérèse looks at the informer. It's unusual for the differences to be so obvious as they are this evening. Dizzying. This man used to go to the rue des Saussaies, used to go up the stairs, knock at a certain door, then say he had the description: tall, dark, twenty-six, the address, the times. He was given an envelope. He said, "Thank you, monsieur," then went off to have an apéritif in the Cafè Les Capitales.

Thérèse says, "You were told to hurry up."

The informer looks up. Then, after a pause, in a small voice intended to sound childlike:

"I'm being as quick as I can, I really am . . . But why—"

He stops short. He used to go into the building in the rue des Saussaies. Without having to wait, ever. The inside of his collar is dirty. He never had to wait, never. Or if he did, he was given a chair, as if he were visiting friends. His shirt is dirty under his white collar. An informer. The two young men snatch his underpants away from him. He trips and falls down in a corner of the room with a thud, like a big parcel.

Roger has hardly spoken to her since their argument

over the German prisoners. And there are others, it's not only Roger.

In the distance, the last snipers on the roofs. It's over. The war has left Paris behind. Everywhere, in doorways, streets, hotel rooms—crowds, joy. Everywhere, girls like her with the soldiers recently landed. And everywhere many others for whom it's all over, for whom there's nothing but idle sadness. But for her it's not over. Neither joy nor the gentle sadness of the end are possible. Her job is to be here, alone with the informer and the two from Montluc, shut up with them in this closed room.

Now he's naked. It's the first time in her life that she's been with a naked man for any other purpose than making love. He's standing, leaning on the chair, his eyes lowered. Waiting. There are others who would agree with her, to begin with these two, these two comrades, and there are bound to be others, others who've waited and not yet been rewarded and who are still waiting and who've forgotten what freedom is because they're still waiting.

Now all his things are on the chair. He's trembling. Shivering. He's afraid. Afraid of us. Of us who were afraid. Of those who had been afraid he was in great fear.

Now he is naked.

"Your glasses!" says Albert.

He takes them off and puts them down on his things. He has old, shriveled testicles, level with the table. He's fat and pink in the gleam of the hurricane lamp. He smells of unwashed flesh. The two young men wait.

"Three hundred francs for a prisoner of war, wasn't it?"

The informer whimpers for the first time.

"And how much for a Jew?"

"You've made a mistake, I tell you . . ."

"What we want," says Thérèse, "is for you to tell us where Albert of the Capitals is, to start with, and then what you did with him and who you saw him with."

He snivels, but without shedding any tears.

"I *told* you I didn't know him from Adam."

The door opens. All the others come in, in silence. The women stand in front, the men behind. It's as if Thérèse were slightly embarrassed to be found in the act of looking at the old man naked. But she can't ask them to leave; there's no reason; they might easily be in her place. She's behind the hurricane lamp. You can see her short black hair and half her white forehead. She is sitting down again.

"Go ahead," says Thérèse. "First we want to know how to find the other one, Albert of the Capitals."

Her voice is unsteady, rather tremulous.

The first blow has fallen, from one of the four arms. It has a strange resonance. The second blow. The informer tries to parry. He bawls, "Ow! Ow! You're hurting me!" Behind him somone laughs and says, "They meant to, believe it or not . . ."

You can see him clearly in the light of the hurricane lamp. The young men are hitting hard. They're punching him in the chest, slowly, hard. While they're hitting him the others, behind, are quiet. They stop hitting him and look at Thérèse again.

"Do you get it now? . . . That's just the beginning," says Lucien.

He rubs his chest and groans quietly.

"Next you've got to tell us how you got into the Gestapo building."

Her voice is jerky, but stronger. Now it's begun, it's well under way, the fellows have been doing a good job. True, it's a serious matter: they're torturing someone. You can disagree, but you can't make fun, or doubt, or be embarrassed.

"Well?"

"Oh . . . the same as everyone else," says the informer.

The group, standing behind him in suspense, relaxes: "Oh . . ."

He whimpers, "You don't actually know . . ." He stops. He rubs his chest, his hands flat. But he's said, "The same as everyone else."

He's said, "The same as everyone else." He thinks they don't actually know. But he didn't say he never went there. You can hear those at the back whispering, "He went there. He said he went there." To the Gestapo, in the rue des Saussaies. Big purple marks are appearing on his chest.

"The same as everyone else, you say? So everyone else went into the Gestapo building?"

In the background: "Swine, traitor, swine." He senses it. He's afraid. He straightens up and tries to see who it's coming from. But there are so many people he can't pick out just one. He too must think he's at the cinema. He hesitates, then pulls himself together.

"You had to show your identity card and leave it on the ground floor. You collected it as you went out."

In the background again: "Bastard. Traitor. Scum."

"I went there in connection with the black market—I didn't think I was doing anything wrong. I've always been very patriotic, just like you. I used to sell them rubbish. Now . . . perhaps I shouldn't have, I don't know . . ."

His voice is still whining, childish. Blood has begun to flow. The skin of his chest has been broken. He seems not to notice. He's afraid.

There was another murmur in the background when he mentioned the black market: "Traitor, pig, bastard." Roger has come in. He's among those in the rear. He too says, "Traitor!" Thérèse recognizes his voice.

"Go on," says Thérèse.

They're not hitting at random. They may not know how to interrogate someone, but they do know how to beat him up. They do it cleverly. They slow down when it looks as though he's going to say something. They start up again as soon as he seems to be recovering.

"What color was the identity card that got you into the Gestapo?"

The two young men smile. Those in the rear too. Even those who don't know what the color was think it's a shrewd question. They've been hitting hard. His eye has been damaged, there's blood on his face. He's crying. The mucus running from his nose is streaked with blood. He keeps moaning, "Ow, ow, oh, oh . . ." He's not answering any more. The skin on his chest is broken over the ribs. He keeps rubbing himself with his hands and smearing himself with blood. With his glassy, elderly, myopic gaze he stares unseeingly at the hurricane lamp. It's happened. It happened very quickly; whether he dies or survives no longer depends on Thérèse. That's of no importance now. He's become someone without anything in common with other men. And with every minute the difference grows bigger and more established.

"You were asked the color of your identity card."

Albert is right up against his nose. A whisper: "Perhaps that's enough . . ."

It's a woman's voice coming out of the dark.

The two young men stop. They turn around and look for her. Thérèse has turned around too.

"Enough?" says Lucien.

"For an informer?" says Albert.

"Even so," says the woman. Her voice is unsteady.

They start again.

"For the last time," says Thérèse, "we asked you the color of the identity card you used to show in the rue des Saussaies."

In the background: "They're going to keep on . . . I'm leaving." A woman again.

"Me too."

Another woman. Thérèse turns around: "Anyone who doesn't like it doesn't have to stay."

Women can be heard vaguely protesting, but they don't leave.

"That's enough!"

It's a man, one of those standing in the rear.

The women stop whispering. Still all that's visible of Thérèse is her white forehead, and sometimes, when she leans forward, her eyes.

But now it's not the same. There's a split in the solidarity of the group. Something decisive is happening. Something new. Approved of by some, disapproved of by others. Some follow ever more closely. Others are becoming strangers. There's no time for fine distinctions: the women are with the informer, the informer is with all those who don't approve. The desire to strike increases with the number of enemies, strangers.

"Come on, quick—the color!"

The two begin hitting again. They hit the places hit before. The informer cries out. When they thump him his cries become strangled, a sort of obscene gurgle. A noise that makes you want to hit even harder, to stop it. He tries to parry the blows, but he can't see them. They all land.

"Well . . . the same as any other identity card . . ."

"Go on."

They hit harder and harder. It doesn't matter. They're indefatigable. They hit better and better, more coolly. The more they hit and the more he bleeds, the more it's clear that hitting is necessary, right, just. Images arise out of the blows. Thérèse is invaded, spellbound by images. A man standing against a wall falls. Another. Another. Unendingly. With the five thousand francs he used to buy little things just for himself. Undoubtedly he wasn't an anti-Communist, not even a collaborator, not even anti-Semitic. No. he just "grassed" unconsciously, painlessly, perhaps just to pay for his little solitary luxuries, to make ends meet, without any real need. He's still lying. He must know, know what he won't say, know only that now. If he confessed, if he stopped trying to defend himself, the difference between him and the others would be less complete. But he holds out as long as he can.

"Go to it."

And they do. It's like an efficient machine. But where does it come from, man's ability to strike, to get used to it, to do it as if it were a job, a duty?

"Please! Please! I'm not a traitor!" cries the informer.

He's afraid of dying. But not enough. He still goes on lying. He wants to live. Even lice cling to life. Thérèse gets up. She's anxious, she's afraid it may never be enough. What could they do to him? What new thing could they think of? The man against the wall who fell, he didn't speak either, what a different silence. Against the wall, in a second, his life was reduced to that overwhelming silence. Against the wall the silence —this one *must* speak, the informer, here. But oh God, it will never be enough. And then there are all those who don't give a damn, the women who left just now, and all the pussyfooters and their sarcasms. "Insurrection, purge—don't make us laugh." You have to strike. There will never be any justice in the world unless you—yourself are justice now. Judges, paneled courtrooms play-acting, not justice. They sang the "Internationale" as they were driven in police vans through the streets, and the bourgeoisie looked out from behind their curtains and said, "Terrorists!" You have to strike. Smash. Shatter the lie. The vile silence. Flood everything with light. Extract the truth this swine has in his gullet. Truth, justice. For what? To kill him? What's the use? But it's not just him. It doesn't concern him. It's just so as to find out. Beat him till he ejaculates his truth, his shame, his fear, the secret of what made him only yesterday all-powerful, inaccessible, untouchable.

Every blow rings out in the silent room. They're hitting at all the traitors, at the women who left, at all those who didn't like what they saw from behind the shutters. The informer yells "ooh, ooh," in long wails. Beyond him, in the shadow, they're silent while the blows are falling. It's when they hear his voice protesting that the insults burst forth, through clenched teeth, with clenched fists. No long phrases. Just the same insults always when the informer's voice shows he's still holding out. For of all the informer's power this remains—this voice, lying. He's still lying. He still has the strength. He hasn't reached the point where he stops lying. Thérèse looks at the fists falling, hears the gong of the blows, realizes for the first time that in a man's body there are layers almost impossible to pierce. Tier upon tier of deep truths difficult to reach. She remembers she'd vaguely realized this during the tireless questioning of a couple, earlier. But not so strongly. Now it's exhausting, almost impossible. Demolition work. Blow by blow. You have to hold out, stick it out. And then, soon, there will emerge, quite small, hard as a seed, the truth. The work is going on far away, in that solitary chest of his. They hit him in the stomach. The informer howls, clutches his stomach with both hands, writhes. Albert draws closer, deals him a blow in the private parts. He covers his genitals with both hands and howls some more. He's bleeding copiously from the face. He wasn't like other men even before. He was an informer, a betrayer of men. He didn't bother to find out why he was asked to do it. Even those who paid him weren't his friends. But now you can't compare him with anything that's alive. Even when he's dead he won't be like a dead man. He'll clutter up the hall. Perhaps it's a waste of time. We ought to make an end of it. There's no point in killing him. And there's no longer any point in letting him live. He's no longer good for anything. He's completely useless. And just because there's no point in killing him, we can go ahead and do it.

"Stop."

Thérèse stands up and walks over to the informer. Her voice sounds rather weak after the hollow boom of the blows. They must get it over with. The men in the background let her get on with it. They leave it to her, don't offer any advice. "Swine, traitor." The brotherly litany of insults fills her with warmth. In the room, silence. The two young men look inquiringly at Thérèse. Everyone is waiting.

"One last time,'" says Thérèse. "We want to know the color of your card. One last time."

The informer looks at her. She's quite close to him. He's not tall. She's almost the same size as he is. But she's slim and young. She's just said, "One last time." His moans have stopped short.

"What do you want me to say?"

She's small. She doesn't want anything. She's calm, and feels a calm rage telling her to shout out calmly the words of a necessity as powerful as one of the elements. She is justice, justice such as there hasn't been on this soil for a hundred and fifty years.

"We want you to tell us the color of the card that let you into the Gestapo."

He starts to snivel again. A strange smell comes off his body, sickening, sweetish—the small of unwashed fat flesh mixed with the smell of blood.

"I don't know, I don't know—I'm innocent, I tell you."

The insults start up again. "Swine, traitor, scum." Thérèse sits down again. A moment's pause. The insults continue. Thérèse says nothing. For the first time someone standing in the rear says, "The only thing to do is liquidate him. Let's get it over with."

The informer looks up. Silence. The informer is afraid. He falls silent too. He opens his mouth. Looks at them. Then a thin, childish moan comes out of his throat.

"If I just knew what you wanted of me . . ." says the informer. He'd like his voice to sound like a pure supplication, but he still makes it sound cunning.

The two young men are sweating. They wipe their brows with their bloody hands. They look at Thérèse.

"It's not enough yet," says Thérèse.

The two young men turn toward the informer, their fists up. Thérèse jumps up and says, "Don't stop any more. Then he'll tell."

An avalanche of blows. It's the end. In the rest of the room, silence again. Thérèse shouts, "Perhaps the card was red?"

The blood is trickling. He's yelling at the top of his lungs.

"Red? Say it—red?"

He opens one eye. He stops yelling. He is going to realize that this time it's the end.

"Red?"

The two young men pull him out of the corner he keeps taking refuge in. They pull him out and throw him back again as if he were a ball.

"Red?"

He doesn't answer. It's as if he were trying to work out what to say.

"Go to it, boys—harder. Red? Quick—red?"

They've hit him on the nose. A spurt of blood. A cry from the informer: "No . . ."

The boys laugh. So does Thérèse.

"Yellow? Yellow, like ours?"

Now he tries to take refuge in the corner again. Every time the boys pull him out and he falls back into it again with a dull thud.

Thérèse has stood up.

"No . . . not . . . yellow."

The men go on. He's choking. He cries out again. His cries are punctuated by the blows. Now the rhythm of the questions and the rhythm of the blows are the same, furious but steady. He still doesn't speak. It's as if he'd stopped thinking of anything. His bloody eyes are wide open, staring at the hurricane lamp.

"If it wasn't yellow, what was it?"

He still doesn't speak. But he has heard; he looks at Thérèse. He's stopped yelling. Both hands are pressed to his belly, he's bent in two. He doesn't try to ward off the blows any more.

"Quick," says Thérèse, "what color? Quick . . ."

He starts yelling again. His cries are fainter, lower. We're coming to an end, but we don't know what end. Perhaps he won't say anything more, but anyway we're coming to the end.

"It was . . . ? It was . . . ? Quick . . . ?"

As if to a child.

They throw him back and forth to one another like a ball, kicking, punching. They're dripping with sweat.

"Stop."

Thérèse goes over to the informer. She's gathered herself together as if to spring. The informer sees her. Draws back. Silence again. He's not even suffering. It's just terror.

"If you tell, we'll leave you alone. If you don't we'll finish you off here and now. Go to it."

Perhaps the informer no longer remembers what we want of him. But he's going to talk. Or so we think. We must remind him of what it's all about. He tries to lift up his head, like a drowning man trying to breathe. He's going to talk. For sure. We've done it. No. It's the blows that stop him from talking. But if the blows stop, he won't talk. Everyone's waiting with bated breath for this delivery, not only Thérèse. It'll soon be the end now. Whatever happens. But he still doesn't talk.

Thérèse cries out.

"All right, I'll tell you what color your card was."

She's helping him. She really has the feeling that she must help him, that he won't manage it now on his own. She says again, "I'll tell you."

The informer starts to shriek. One long shriek like a siren. They don't leave him time to speak. And the shriek stops short. "Green . . ." shouts the informer.

Silence. The boys stop. The informer looks at the hurricane lamp. He's stopped moaning. He looks completely lost. He's collapsed on the floor. He may have talked. Perhaps he's wondering how he talked. Silence in the background. Thérèse sits down. It's over.

"Yes," says Thérèse. "It was green."

As if stating something known for centuries. It's over.

D. comes over to Thérèse. He offers her a cigarette. She smokes. The informer is still in his corner, petrified.

"Get dressed," says Thérèse.

But he doesn't. The two boys are having a cigarette too. D. has held out a cigarette to the informer. He doesn't see it.

"The cards issued to agents of the German Secret Police were green," says Thérèse.

On the other side of the room the comrades are beginning to stir. Some leave.

"And what about Albert of the Capitals?" says someone on the other side of the room.

Thérèse looks at D. It's true. There's still Albert of the Capitals.

"We'll see," says D. "We'll see tomorrow."

It doesn't seem to interest him any more. He takes Thérèse's hand, helps her to stand. They go out. Albert and Lucien help the informer to dress.

In the bar there's a bright light belonging to another world. Electric light. All the women are there, five of them, and the two men who left when they did.

"He confessed," Thérèse tells them.

No one answers. Thérèse understands. They don't give a damn about his having confessed. She sits down and looks at them. It's strange. They must have been here for half an hour or more. What were they doing here in the bar? What were they waiting for? They came to take refuge in the light.

"He confessed," Thérèse says again.

None of the five looks at her. One women gets up and says carelessly, still without looking at her, "So fucking what?"

D., who was beside Thérèse, goes over to the woman. "Fucking well leave her alone, can't you?"

Roger and D. put their arms around Thérèse. The women say nothing. They go out. The two men who are with them go out too, whistling.

"And you're going home to get some sleep," says D.

"Yes."

Thérèse picks up a glass of wine and drinks.

She can feel D. looking at her. The wine is bitter. She sets the glass down.

"We must let him go," says Thérèse. "He can walk."

Roger isn't sure we ought to let him go.

"We don't want to set eyes on him again," says Thérèse.

"They won't want to lose a catch like that," says Roger.

"I'll explain," says D.

Thérèse starts to cry.

In the morning D. said, "We'll have to take Ter to Beaupain's."

Thérèse didn't ask why. D. deals with all sorts of things: arrests, prisoners, supplies for the group, requisitioning of premises, requisitioning of cars, requisitioning of gas, interrogations. The Richelieu center is packed. Eleven members of the Militia, including Ter, in the cashier's office. Thirty collaborators in the hall. Downstairs the RNP*; a German woman; an agent from the rue des Saussaies; a housemaid and her mistress, who is a writer; a Russian colonel; some journalists; a poet; a lawyer's wife; and so on. So it's probably to make more room in the cashier's office that D. wants to take Ter to the rue de la Chaussée d'Antin, headquarters of the Hernandez-Beaupain group.

So Thérèse has driven D. and Ter to Beaupain's in the rue de la Chaussée d'Antin. It's three in the afternoon. As always, they hear the Spaniards yelling as they go into the building. The courtyard is crowded with bicycles and cars requisitioned or taken from the Germans. Today there's a new one, a gray delivery truck.

The Hernandez-Beaupain group works from the ground floor of a building overlooking two courtyards.

---

* RNP: *Rassemblement National Populaire* (National People's Rally), a right-wing collaborationist group.

The first is connected to the street by a passage belonging to the block as a whole; the second, which is very small, is separated by iron railings from some other courtyards. These two courtyards are connected by a corridor that runs through the ground floor. As soon as you reach the first courtyard you can hear the Spaniards shouting in the huge empty ground floor.

Beaupain is standing at the entrance to the corridor. He's a tall fellow with long arms, long legs, a small head, and the shoulders of a giant. He's got a handsome face with gentle, childlike blue eyes. D. passes quite close to Beaupain, giving a nod as he goes by. Beaupain's manner is strange. He doesn't say hello to D. He keeps looking first toward the street and then toward the other end of the corridor. Now something's happening at the end of the corridor.

There are snatches of shouting in Spanish. Beaupain looks uneasy.

D., Ter, and Thérèse stop at the entrance to the corridor. There's something unusual going on. Silhouetted against the sun in the little courtyard beyond, a group of about fifteen men are waving their arms and talking loudly in Spanish. D., Ter, and Thérèse don't go any farther but stay where they are and look, like Beaupain. The group of men starts to separate, the men draw apart from one another, and then you can see what it was they were crowding around. It's something white. White and stretched out on the ground. The men line up on either side of it along the corridor. Two of them get hold of it, pick it up, and begin to carry it away.

D., Ter, and Thérèse leave Beaupain where he is and advance a little way into the corridor. The corpse is carried past them. The corridor is quiet, the Spaniards are silent. Two suede shoes stick out from under the sheet, two almost new shoes neatly laced up over blue socks. The thing is soft and wobbles like jelly with every step the bearers take. The belly is higher than the feet because the hands have been folded over it. Beneath the sheet you can see the shape of the head, the tip of the nose.

D. goes up to the group of Spaniards who have stayed behind at the end of the corridor. Thérèse and Ter follow him. He touches one of them on the arm and asks who it is.

"A traitor."

The man moves away to join the rest of the Spaniards in the courtyard.

D., Thérèse, and Ter go back quickly to the other end of the corridor, overlooking the courtyard, preceded by all the Spaniards. The bearers have laid the body down on the steps at the foot of the stairs. The gray truck that was in the yard backs up toward them. The two doors at the back are opened, the two men put the body inside. The two feet in their suede shoes come uncovered and you can see the ends of a pair of navy blue trousers. The two men slam the doors of the truck, which starts up right away, drives out through the passage, and disappears into the street.

At once the Spaniards start shouting again. They surge back into the corridor and then into the apartment. D., Ter, and Thérèse go after them. Beaupain is among them. D. asks again who it is. Same answer: "A traitor."

The Spaniards' room is large, paneled, and completely bare. Not a chair. Not a picture. Only, in the four corners, piles of guns with a man watching over them. There's a magnificent fireplace of white marble surmounted by a mirror six feet high. But nothing on the mantelpiece, not a single thing. The Spaniards sleep and eat in here. All they possess, apart from their guns, is in their pockets. So the room is bare and full of men who haven't changed their clothes for a fortnight—light, agile, completely fined down by fighting.

D. is looking for Beaupain. Thérèse and Ter follow him into the adjoining room, which serves as an office both for Gauthier and for the French. Apart from Gauthier's chair and desk there's no furniture in here either. Beaupain is here, arguing with Gauthier. Twenty or so men sit leaning against the walls and listening. From time to time they start yelling and drown Beaupain's and Gauthier's voices. They're yelling because there isn't any wine and all they have to eat is tuna fish sandwiches. D. and Beaupain found a thousand cans of tuna fish in a German post on the first day of the insurrection. Since then the eighty men at the Richelieu center and the sixty men at the Chaussée d' Antin center have been eating nothing but tuna fish. Seventeen days—the men are fed up with tuna fish. Beaupain is berating Gauthier. Gauthier says he brought back a big wheel of Gruyère cheese that he found in an abandoned German truck at Levallois. He says the cheese was still in the truck yesterday evening. And the truck was still in the courtyard. And now all that's left is the truck. The Gruyère—gone. The men start to yell. They think Gauthier's accusing them of having stolen the cheese. Beaupain stamps out in disgust. D. catches him by the arm and asks who it is.

"An agent of the Gestapo. From the Campagne Première center. The Hernandez group got him."

"Where? How?"

"Three revolver shots in the back of the neck. Here, in the courtyard."

Beaupain leaves. D. and Thérèse make for the courtyard. A yard or so from the door, on a slightly hollow flagstone, there's some blood congealing. It glistens in the sun. There's a tree growing close by. There's no one at the windows overlooking the courtyard; most of them are shut. The courtyard is empty.

"Why the blood on the stone?" asks Thérèse.

D. doesn't answer. D. and Thérèse remain in the doorway, looking at the blood. This is the first execution. The first time.

Beaupain goes by again. And, though D. hasn't asked any questions, "He sniveled," says Beaupain.

He goes on his way. He must be looking for the people who stole the cheese. Then along comes Gauthier. He's searching too. For Beaupain.

"Were you there?" asks D.

"No. Where's Beaupain?"

We don't know. Pierrot comes up and asks D. for a cigarette, takes one, and lights up. Pierrot's a youngster, about eighteen.

"Looking, eh?" says Pierrot.

"Were you there?" asks D.

"I'll say I was!" says Pierrot. "He sniveled disgustingly, said he'd do anything we wanted if we'd let him go, said he realized now."

He also said the Spaniards had argued among themselves. Over who would get to shoot him. They were still arguing about it, he said. Finally it was Hernandez and two others who all did it together with an 8 mm in the back of the neck.

Pierrot leaves. D. and Thérèse go back into the Spaniards' room. A group is wrangling heatedly in the middle of the room. Others take no part in the argument and are sitting on the floor along the walls, dismantling and greasing their guns.

Ter is leaning against the fireplace. Yes, Ter. Ter of the Militia. He's pale. Not in the same way as Beaupain just now; differently. Ter's nose is pinched and he's turned green; his lips are like chalk and he's gray under the eyes. It's true, we'd forgotten about Ter. Forgotten him for about ten or fifteen minutes. He's seen the stretcher go by; through the doorway overlooking the inner courtyard he's seen the blood on the stone. No one thought about Ter seeing these things. Certainly none of the Spaniards. And not even Thérèse, not even D.

And now, lo and behold, we find Ter leaning against the fireplace, all on his own. D. goes over. And as soon as Ter sees him coming (he must have been waiting for this to happen from the start), his face goes tense and literally writhes toward D., though he doesn't stop leaning against the fireplace. D. goes right up to Ter, who tries to talk to him. Ter's voice is very faint.

"I'd like to write a note to my family," says Ter.

D. and Thérèse look at each other. They'd forgotten Ter. And now they know he's seen the stretcher go by and seen the blood through the doorway. D. looks intently at Ter, goes on looking. Then gives him a smile.

"No," says D., "we didn't bring you here to execute you."

Ter looks up at D. That look, that movement of Ter's eyes toward D., the force that made his eyelids lift and look at D. . . . .

"Oh!" says Ter. "Because I'd have liked to know."

"No," says D., "don't worry."

Ter's eyelids and his head fall back heavily. And Ter says nothing more. Nor does he move. He stays propped on his elbows, leaning against the fireplace, his body slightly slanted. D. leans against the fireplace, near Ter. He's still gazing at him. So is Thérèse. Men and more men go by. Ter's eyes are lowered. Now the men are arguing about the Gruyére. Gauthier is running after Beaupain. Beaupain has had enough of Gauthier for the moment. He goes from one Spaniard to another asking who has seen the Gruyère. Gruyère? No one's set eyes on it. Gauthier is following Beaupain around, grinning as if he knew something. Every so often there's a great roar of laughter. Still about the cheese.

The men sit in the corners carefully greasing their guns. Some of them are eating: the French, tuna fish sandwiches; the Spaniards, tuna fish sandwiches and tomatoes. The Spaniards always have tomatoes in their pockets and eat them all day long. No one knows where or how they get hold of them.

D. takes out his cigarette pack and holds it under

Ter's nose. Ter's hand flicks up and takes a cigarette. "Thanks," says Ter. D. offers Thérèse a cigarette too. He takes one himself, then offers Ter a light. When he sees the flame, Ter looks up again at D. D. smiles. Ter gives a very brief smile too, then looks down again, still leaning against the fireplace. He smokes the cigarette with all his might, inhaling in great gulps.

Beaupain gets all the men together and tells them about the mysterious disappearance of the cheese. It's inexplicable, says Beaupain, a whole Gruyère weighing thirty kilos doesn't just walk away on its own. The men listen, smile, and start arguing again. Still no one's set eyes on any Gruyère. Beaupain is dripping with sweat, he's yelling and he's getting tired. And he gives orders about where the various groups are to sleep that night. When he's finished a Spaniard comes up to him and says a few words. Beaupain immediately remembers something, and asks everyone at large who has taken the Bren gun that was still on his desk yesterday evening; and the two submachine guns that disappeared that morning—one belongs to the group, the other to a little FAI,* the one who just spoke to him. The little FAI nods his head indignantly. No one has seen either the submachine guns or the Bren. The little FAI goes from one group to another asking the same question, "Have you seen the submachine gun?" and holding out his empty hands. No one has seen it.

Ter is still smoking. D. and Thérèse can't help watching him smoke.

* FAI: Fédération Anarchiste Ibérique (Federation of Spanish Anarchists), mostly veterans of the Spanish Civil War.

Ter is twenty-three. A handsome young man. He's not wearing a jacket, and you can see the muscles in his long young forearms. He has a narrow waist and his leather belt is drawn tight. He isn't pale now. But he's still smoking fiercely, drawing hard on his cigarette. He has a nine-day beard. A blue silk shirt. Suede shoes. His belt's made of raw pigskin. If it wasn't for the silk, the suede, and the belt you might take him for a member of the group. But Ter has an unsavory past. It's no good—he has. Upon Ter's young life has grown the horrific past of which he is likely to die.

D. and Thérèse look at him. He's smoking, eyes lowered. The hand holding the cigarette is shaking, the other is holding on to the fireplace. From time to time Ter looks up, sees D., and smiles like someone apologizing.

In all the corners men grease their guns and talk about the stolen submachine guns, the Gruyère, the Gestapo agent.

D. goes on taking no notice of anything but Ter of the Militia. Twenty-three. He's wasted his life. He made friends with Lafont; Lafont impressed him with his bullet-proof car, his bullet-proof door and walls. Ter's a funny fellow. He hasn't a thought in his head, only desires; he's got a body made for pleasure, riotous living, fighting, girls. A week ago D. and Roger interrogated him. Thérèse was present. Those who were there know him as well as if they'd known him always.

Ter had been a friend of the Bony-Lafont gang.

"Why did you go into the Militia?" he was asked.

"It was the only way to get a gun . . ."

"Why did you want a gun?"

"It impresses people."

They plagued him for an hour to find out what he did with his gun and how many members of the Resistance he'd killed with it.

"I was the lowest of the low in the gang—I wouldn't have been allowed to kill any members of the Resistance."

He said he'd gone hunting in the Sologne with some movie actors. For a while he'd been Lafont's secretary. He didn't say he wouldn't have killed some members of the Resistance if he could.

He'd been found out by an FFI group* in the fifteenth arrondissement that he'd managed to get into, and because they hadn't enough room to keep him themselves, they'd handed him over to the Richelieu group. They'd asked him, "What the hell were you doing in the FFI?"

"I wanted to fight."

"What with?"

"My gun."

"You mean you thought that was the only way to hide?"

"No, I wanted to fight. It wasn't that I wished the Germans any harm. I just wanted to fight."

They had found an FFI armband in his pocket. They

---

* FFI: Forces Françaises de l'Intérieur (French Forces of the Interior), a grouping together of domestic resistance organizations in spring 1944, which, along with the FFL (Forces Françaises Libres), who had operated from the UK, etc., with the Allies, now made up the army of the French Provisional Government.

asked him what he was doing with it there. He said he'd found it. He smiled: "I ask you! A guy like me wearing an armband?"

Beaupain goes by, still looking for the Bren gun and the Gruyère.

"Can I speak to you when you have a minute?" says D.

"Go ahead," says Beaupain.

They move away to have a talk. Thérèse stays with Ter by the fireplace. She thinks Beaupain and D. must be talking about Ter, but that he doesn't suspect it. In fact, he is beginning to enjoy himself. He watches the group of Spaniards cleaning their guns, and D. and Beaupain talking, but especially the Spaniards. That's Ter all over. He's thrown away his life in order to drive a car and have a revolver in his pocket. He went on the spree with Lafont and Bony. He drove Lafont's armored car hell for leather when Lafont raided the Jewish quarters. One day, going hunting, he shot into the trees, he doesn't know whether he killed anyone. We know all about him. He confessed everything right away.

For Ter, everything is simple. He says to himself, "I had a gun, I was in Lafont's gang, I shot into the trees, I'm going to be executed." Anyone who's done wrong has to be executed. It's no use making excuses, thinks Ter. He bows to the demands of justice and of society. He believes in the wisdom of judges, in the law, in punishment. And meanwhile it's amusing to watch guns being dismantled, click, clack. He's like a plant, is Ter. Like a kind of child.

Thérèse and D. have rather a soft spot for Ter. It's inevitable. Inevitable that you should feel drawn to some people and repelled by others. At the Richelieu center there's a man of the world much less guilty than Ter, and who knew he'd get off. Not Ter—he's sure he's going to be shot. The man of the world asked to be put with people "of his own kind" because "he had a right to some respect." So D. put him in the communal cubicle in the hall with a prize wrestler and a housemaid.

Ter made six million in one year in a German purchasing office.*

"How much did you earn?"

"Six million in 1943, two million this year."

He didn't hesitate for a second before he told us. He really hasn't a scrap of cunning or pride. What he'd like more than anything else is some cigarettes. And a woman. While he was being questioned, a week after his arrest, he kept looking at Thérèse. He's got the look of a wolf and fast liver, and he must miss the girls. And though his mistress is down in the hall she can't be allowed to come up. It's forbidden. There are already eleven people in the cashier's office, and anyway it's not possible. Prisoners are not allowed to have it. Like cigarettes.

D. has rejoined Ter and Thérèse.

"We're leaving . . ."

* In addition to making official industrial purchases from French manufacturers, Germany also bought materials and equipment (at higher prices) through offices dealing in goods held back from official transactions.

Ter walks on in front. D. leans over to Thérèse and whispers, "Beaupain hasn't any room. We'll have to phone Cherche-Midi."

As they go out D. gives a friendly wave to Hernandez. So does Thérèse. Hernandez is a giant of a man, a Communist, it was he and two of his group who executed the agent. There are seventeen in the group, and all the French look on them as their seniors in the matter of fighting. The fact that Hernandez undertook the agent's execution probably makes D. and Thérèse think they were right to put their trust in him. It was quite in order for his group to do the job. The agent was a Frenchman, but the French hadn't made any objection; maybe they weren't sure he ought to be executed. Hernandez was. Hernandez is eating some tomatoes, his smile is like that of a huge child. He's a hairdresser by trade, a Spanish Republican by dedication. And with the same ease and certainty he'd blow his own brains out if it would help to bring about the Spanish revolution. When they're not fighting, the Spaniards spend their time greasing the guns they've managed to get hold of. They know where to find them, they stay away all night, they sleep very little, they talk on and on endlessly about the coming fight in Spain. They all expect to set out in the next few days. "Now it's Franco's turn," Hernandez always says. It keeps them awake at night; the Liberation of Paris is the Spaniards' inspiration. The great thing for them is to get hold of enough guns and regroup. But the Socialists set conditions that are unacceptable to the Communists and the FAI. The latter want to regroup independently on the Spanish frontier. The Socialists want to form an expeditionary force in Paris. All day long they talk about going to Spain. They've all thrown up their jobs to go back.

Going past Hernandez, Thérèse thinks that if Ter had to be executed in the next few days it would be best if he, Hernandez, did it. She'd rather it was Hernandez. She smiles at him. Only Hernandez knows so well why it's necessary to kill him. She doesn't know the details about what D. and Beaupain said to each other about Ter of the Militia. Questions of organization, no doubt. Ter is going to leave the center; perhaps he's going to be executed.

Ter is glad to be leaving the d'Antin center. He strides along swiftly in front of D. and Thérèse. He knows he's going back to the cashier's office at the Richelieu center, but he doesn't think about that for the moment. The prospect of the ride from the d'Antin center to the Richelieu center makes him forget. That's Ter—it doesn't take much to make him forget.

In the street, by the car, Ter suddenly moves away from D. and Thérèse, walks around the car, and sweeps open the door for Thérèse with a courtly gesture and a smile. It's true he's glad to be leaving the d'Antin center, but it's not just that. It's that he likes Thérèse and D. It's that Thérèse is driving, that he used to drive, and he feels a sort of affinity with her. Ter is not an ordinary prisoner. For an extraordinary thing happened while he was being questioned: he was so impressed with D.'s fairness that his total, almost disconcerting confession was undoubtedly due in part to a wish to please him. That's Ter—simple. He's like a sort of plant, is Ter.

Ter is sitting beside Thérèse, who's driving. D. is in the back seat. In his right hand he's holding a little old small-caliber revolver, the only weapon he's got left: his Bren and his 8 mm were stolen at the Richelieu center. The revolver D. is holding is jammed, it hasn't worked for a long time. D. found it in his desk drawer, where the 8 mm had been. There was no way of knowing where it came from. Thérèse too knows that the revolver trained on Ter doesn't work. Ter doesn't know, of course. He may have noticed that the revolver is ridiculously small, but he's too impressed by D. to suspect it doesn't work. For Ter, D. can only own weapons as perfect as his soul.

Ter sits quietly beside Thérèse.

It's a fine, bright day. No police. The police fought with the people of Paris and haven't resumed their normal functions since the Liberation. For three days there haven't been any police in the streets. Cars full of FFI drive about in all directions, even up no-entry streets, going extremely fast and swerving onto the sidewalk to pass. People are drunk with freedom, overcome by a frenzy of disobedience.

Ter is fascinated by the speed and the number of cars, by the guns protruding through their windows and shining in the sun.

"Have to make the most of it," D. says suddenly. "No police yet. It happens only once in a lifetime."

Ter turns around to look at D., who is holding the revolver trained on him. And he laughs. "You're right."

That's Ter—pleased because there are no policemen around. He's never liked the police. The reason he feels so much at home with D. is that D. doesn't belong to the police. Ter doesn't think, it doesn't occur to him that the fact of there not being any policemen around heralds a new era, an era he won't know. He doesn't think ahead, Ter.

Ter is very interested in the gears, the acceleration, and the steering in the sunny bustle of the streets. He likes handling cars, guns, money, women. He likes anything that goes, makes a noise, is lavish. For him, the handling of a car is something fascinating in itself. Especially as it's such a change from the life he's been leading for the last eleven days in the cashier's office, with the ten other members of the Militia. It really is a lovely day, and all these cars full of young men and girls the same age as Ter, driving full tilt with machine guns and rifles aimed in all directions, make the summer more intriguing and intense. All this free, excited, victorious chaos has a long-distance effect upon Ter, who's happy to be in one of the cars and a part of all the activity, in no matter what capacity.

It's probably the last ride of Ter's life.

At each turn, carefully, punctiliously, Ter sticks out his arm to help. To help with the driving of the car taking him straight back to his cell in the Richelieu center, from which he'll probably never emerge again except in a police van.

Every so often there comes from the roofs of the houses the rattle of machine guns, background to bright sun and green leaves. When it's too close the passersby huddle in doorways and laugh at the FFI going by in their cars.

And at one point Thérèse turns and winks at D. over

the jammed revolver. And D. and Thérèse smile. Only Ter is serious. He conscientiously puts out his arm at every turn.

When Thérèse and Albert took Ter back to his cell, Ter asked Thérèse whether it might be possible to have some extra bread over and above the ration, and also a pack of cards to pass the time. He asked Thérèse this, in a whisper, so that Albert wouldn't hear.

D. went to the kitchen to have it out with the FFI, who were pilfering from the prisoners' rations, and Thérèse went to get a pack of cards and some bread.

In the late afternoon Thérèse went with Albert to the cashier's office to give Ter the cards and the bread. Ter was sitting on the table telling the other prisoners about his drive through Paris. Thérèse gave him the cards and the bread.

And in the evening they found Ter sitting on the table and surrounded by three other members of the Militia. They were playing cards.

The others didn't really want to play, they played without enthusiasm. Ter made them play. Ter had a real urge to play, the urge of someone who's going to live, no less. He was sitting cross-legged on the table, forcing the others to choose cards and then play them. Then he played his own. On his own. He threw the cards down on the table and was delighted when he won. Wham! Ace! Trumps! My trick!

Beside Ter on the table was a bit of bread. All that was left of the three loaves Thérèse had brought him. They'd eaten the lot. Ter had shared.

Even Albert had a soft spot for Ter—Albert, who

was so fierce with all the others. One day when Ter was down in the hall, D. found him deep in conversation with Albert. Albert was sitting in a leather armchair. Ter was sitting at his feet.

"Tell me—about women? How many have you had?"

Ter thought.

"In how long?" he asked.

"The last year—how many in the last year?"

"Three hundred and ninety-five."

Then Ter and Albert split their sides, and so did D., who'd just come in. All three of them together.

Ter was incorrigible. Even if he was to die the next day, he wouldn't have missed an opportunity to live. Ter was convinced he was contemptible because D. had told him so, and you had to believe D. Ter was without pride, he had nothing in his head, nothing but childhood.

We never knew whether he was shot, or whether he survived. If he survived he must have belonged to the section of society where money comes easily and goes easily, where ideas are in short supply, and where the mystique of the leader is the only form of ideology and excuses crime.

THE CRUSHED NETTLE

This one is invented. Literature.

I was probably in the French Communist Party at the time, because the story's about a class confrontation. It wasn't bad, but it was unpublishable. I've been lucky in that I have always unconsciously preserved my writing from the nauseating proximity of the Communist Party to which I once belonged. Fortunately, this text has remained unpublished for forty years. I have rewritten it. Now I can't remember what it's about. But it's a text that takes off on its own. It might work well in the movies.

Sometimes I think the stranger is Ter of the Militia, who's escaped from the Richelieu center and is looking for somewhere to die. It might be the light-colored suit that makes me think that, the light-colored leather shoes, the white skin of Nazi Germany, and the smell of that luxury, the English cigarette.

The stranger sits down on the big paving stones strewn along the sides of the road. They must have been brought here some time ago, perhaps even before the Occupation. Then the idea of laying down sidewalks along this little road must have been abandoned.

On either side of the road there's a row of wooden shacks, with corrugated iron roofs, surrounded by rickety fences on which here and there washing has been hung out to dry. Around the paving stones and in the spaces between them there are nettles and wild convolvulus. They also grow up against the fences around the wooden houses: an invasion. Every so often, in the gardens and along the road, there are some acacias. No other trees.

From the shacks there comes the sound of crockery, voices, the squalling of children, mothers shouting, no words.

Two children go back and forth along the road. The elder might be about ten. He's pushing his little brother up and down in an old stroller between the place where the stranger is sitting and the hole the road leads to. The hole is overgrown with a tangle of old iron and nettles.

Since the stranger turned up the child has shortened his beat, so that he goes past him more often. The younger brother is wearing a blue shirt that's too small for him. His feet are bare, and his fair head flops about on the back of the stroller. He's asleep. His straight hair is tousled, and bits are caught between his closed eyelids. That's where the flies are, in the damp shadow of the lashes. From time to time the elder boy stops and stealthily examines the stranger, with empty but sharp curiosity, chewing a stalk of grass and humming under his breath. He too is barefoot. He's a thin child with full lips and very dark hair, tangled and dull. He's dressed in a little girl's smock, also blue, with a wide-open neck. His head is small and narrow, his eyes still clear and deep. Sometimes his face freezes and he takes fright. That's when he thinks the stranger is looking at *him*. But he soon starts walking up and down again between the shacks.

The stranger has been there ten minutes when the man appears on the road. He sits down on a stone too, not far from the stranger. It's a man who's in the habit of coming here. He must be about fifty. He's wearing a beret shiny with grease. He pulls up his trouser legs to sit down, and his calves are thin and hairy above big black hobnailed boots. He's wearing an army shirt and a gray, rather short jacket. The little boy stops in front of the workman. The child's face has brightened up miraculously, he's smiling. They say hello to each other.

The child wheels the stroller under the acacia on the other side of the road, then comes and sits down beside the man. "Have you had your dinner?" "Yes," says the boy.

Like the boy, the man looks stealthily at the stranger, but he remains quite calm. His face is tanned and dry.

He has blue eyes, this man, eyes that are small and lively—and kind. His cheeks are hollow, he can't have many teeth left.

It's hot, a heavy, sticky heat unrelieved by any breath or stir. The drone you can hear is the flies going from one nettle to another in the heavy air.

The man pulls his knapsack to him and gets out his lunchpail and a bottle of wine. The stranger seems to avoid looking at it. He must know the man is keeping an eye on him, wondering why he's here on this road at the back of beyond, someone who's obviously so much a stranger.

The man gets out his lunchpail, and you can see that the index finger on his left hand is covered by a loose leather stall fastened around the wrist. He opens the pail, holding the finger out so as to keep it from touching anything. The little boy watches him. He seems to have forgotten the stranger for the moment. "Does it still hurt?" he asks. "Not now. I don't bother about it any more."

The pail has haricot beans in it. The man gets a bit of bread out of his bag. He moves slowly. The stranger takes his hat off and puts it down on a nearby stone. He's hot. He's wearing a light-colored suit. Almost white.

The boy watches the man. His face has relaxed. There's a strange eagerness about him, he wants the man to speak. They must be in the habit of meeting. "And your father?" asks the man. "Better," says the boy.

The man wipes his spoon on the lapel of his jacket

and dips it in the pail. He eats. Chews. Eats. Swallows. All with the slow regularity of a performance, of a futile but insidious repetition.

Behind them, behind the stranger, the man, and the child, is the same solid mass of the city. In front of them, the beginning of the nettles. The city ends where the weeds and old iron begin. The war has left it behind. It's all over. The pungent smell comes from another hole—invisible, this one—which must serve as a rubbish dump for the people in the shacks. The flies that are drinking at the baby's eyes come from there. Ever since he was born he's been a prey to the flies from the dump, and has breathed, been steeped in, the smell. Now and then the smell grows fainter, but then it comes back again, horrible, filling the summer.

The man is still eating his beans beneath the gaze of both the boy and the stranger. He takes a mouthful of beans, cuts off a bit of bread with his penknife, and puts it all in his mouth. He chews. Slowly. The elder of the two children watches the man chewing. Shouts, the crying of children, the clatter of crockery can still be heard from the shacks. No words.

A siren sounds in the distance, very sad, like an air-raid alert during the war.

The man puts his piece of bread down on the stone and takes his watch out of his vest pocket. Still slowly, he sets it. He says, "One minute past twelve." He turns toward the stranger: "An awful noise. Still scares you."

The stranger doesn't answer. You might think he was deaf. The man starts eating his beans again. Still with the same excessive, drawn-out slowness, in the

stinking heat of the invisible hole. The boy isn't looking at him any more. He's looking at the stranger, who
didn't answer. He's never seen a stranger before on this
road, a man so very clean and white and fair.

"Where are we?" asks the stranger.

The boy laughs, then looks down, embarrassed. The
man stops chewing. He looks at the stranger. He's sur-
prised too.

"Over there is Petit-Clamart." He points in the direction of the heap of nettles and old iron. "Here it's still
Paris. In theory . . ."

The man is seized with uncertainty.

"Why? Are you lost?"

"Yes." The word rings out.

The boy laughs again, then stops and looks down.
The man has stopped smiling.

He picks up the bottle of wine and a glass. Drinks.
Doesn't say anything.

The stranger must know that the man won't speak
again of his own accord. The stranger speaks; it's not
a question, he says, "You've hurt your finger."

The man lifts up his finger and looks at it.

"I lost a finger, well, almost, the top joint. It got
caught in a press."

For the first time the boy speaks. He blushes and
takes off, saying all in one breath, "His finger was
squashed as flat as a pancake and there was a woman
in the factory too, her whole hand was caught in the
machine, they had to cut it off."

The stranger can't take his eyes off the masticating
mouth. The boy's eyes want to see everything too. He

can't take his eyes off the two men. Again the man speaks.

"They're great big guns," he says. "Two tons . . . And in the ordnance factories they make some that weigh five. Really big things . . ."

The baby utters a cry. Just one. A nightmare. A young woman appears at the door of one of the shacks and calls out, "Marcel!" The little boy gets up and looks at her: "It's nothing." Everyone keeps quiet. The baby goes back to sleep.

The man has finished the beans and gets a piece of cheese out of his bag. He cuts off a little bit and puts it on the bread. He cuts off the bit of bread with the cheese on it. He eats, still in the same slow motion, but it is easy, irresistible. The boy says, "I didn't think you would, but you're going to have just enough bread to go with the cheese."

The boy is uneasy because of the silence of the man eating the cheese. Not because of the silence of the stranger. He looks at the man, Lucien.

"How terrible," says the stranger at last.

The man turns toward him. He's not smiling any more. The boy realizes that the man, Lucien, is beginning to be afraid of something. The stranger says, "And you went back to the same job."

The stranger doesn't think of what he's saying, he's speaking mechanically, of being silent, instead of dying. He has something shut up inside himself that he can't say, can't reveal. Because he doesn't know what it is. He doesn't know how one speaks about death. He is confronted with himself just as the man and the little boy are. The man and the little boy know it. The man is going to speak in the stranger's stead, but he might just as easily refrain from speaking. All these efforts are designed to ward off silence. One thing is certain. If the silence were not warded off by the two men a dangerous phase would open for all of them, the children, the stranger, the man. The first word that occurs to one to describe it is madness.

"Yes, I went back to the same job," says the man. "Last year I was on the riveting. I prefer the press. It's a matter of taste. I find the press less monotonous. Perhaps because it's dangerous. It may be harder, but you've got your own gun, your own machine. I prefer it."

The stranger has started once again to listen without hearing, to look without seeing.

"Sometimes there's more than one person working on the press, too," the man goes on. "But it's quite different—you can see your own gun being made. Whereas the riveting is more . . . what shall I say? . . . more a matter of detail, of finishing. It's less personal. And you're never on your own, you're always working with other people. It's nice to be on your own sometimes."

The man has been speaking with an attempt at formality that delights the little boy. There's no friendliness left in the man now, no kindness. He's talking now to prevent the stranger from speaking. The stranger doesn't answer.

The little boy cries out in a sort of sudden gladness. A gladness not unconnected with the man's new attitude toward the stranger.

The man gives a rather ironical smile, and his blue eyes have gone hard.

"Perhaps you're in the steel business too," he says. "You never know."

The stranger gives a mocking smile too, but doesn't answer. He just says, "No."

There's a slight interruption in the movements of the man who is eating, and silence returns. And the fear grows nearer, more intense. The boy doesn't understand what's going to happen. He feels abandoned.

The man takes one, two, three long swigs of wine. When he's finished he holds the bottle out to the boy.

"Here, have a swig."

The boy drinks and makes a face. He has trouble swallowing the wine. The stranger looks up and says, "You give wine to a child?"

"Yes . . . Why? Any objections?"

The stranger looks at the workman. They look at each other. The stranger says, "No."

The man takes out his watch again, looks at it, and puts it back in his vest pocket. Then he takes out a pack of Gauloises. The baby is awake again. The boy goes over and starts pulling the stroller up and down again behind him, still keeping his eyes on the two men.

The stranger suddenly turns around, as if in a panic. For no apparent reason. Then he resumes his silence. The man says, "I've still got a quarter of an hour—time to smoke a cigarette."

The man holds out his pack of cigarettes to the stranger.

"No, thank you," says the stranger. "I have some on me."

The stranger now takes a pack of cigarettes out of

his pocket. The man holds out a smoky lighter, his hand shaking slightly.

They smoke without saying anything to each other. Then the workman looks as if he's seen something in the distance, in front of him; but no, it's nothing. He smokes, thoroughly at ease. Fear comes and goes. Now it's back again. The man sniffs and says, "You're smoking an English cigarette."

The stranger doesn't answer, he doesn't understand. He says, "What do you mean?"

The man looks at the stranger as the stranger was just now looking at him. He doesn't answer.

The two men are silent. The boy starts to forget about them. He hums a tune from school. The stranger speaks to the man: "Are you happy?"

The man looks at him. "What do you mean?"

The stranger thinks, trying to find out what he does mean. He can't.

"I don't know."

In front of the stranger there is a clump of nettles in flower. It's growing in the middle of the road, in a round bush, full of venom and fire. The stranger leans forward, breaks off a stalk, and crumples it up in his hand. He makes a face, throws the nettle away, and rubs his smarting hands. You can hear the boy laughing. The man has completely stopped smoking. The stranger senses that he's looking at him, he's still leaning over the nettle; then suddenly he makes up his mind, looks up, and speaks. "Sorry," he says.

The boy laughs again. Uncontrollably. The man tells him to be quiet. The boy stops laughing at once, he's afraid the man will send him away. The man says, "Haven't you ever seen nettles before?"

Now the man is angry. His fear has melted away. He's sitting up facing the stranger.

"It's not that," says the stranger. "But I can't recognize them."

The man throws his cigarette away; it falls in a patch of sunlight. He takes out another. He's no longer waiting for the stranger to speak. He seems to have forgotten about going back to work. He doesn't look at the stranger any more. He thinks of him as something that's now in the past, inaccessible and pointless. As for the stranger, he no longer speaks. He's resumed his former attitude, head bowed, staring at death. And the man is instinctively drifting toward the region of death where the stranger is. He says, "I stayed here during the Occupation. Never left the district."

The stranger hasn't moved. The man now walks around him, a few steps, then back again, points at the city. He says, "It's a week now since it ended. Every so often you hear snipers on the roofs. But less and less."

The siren goes again. The boy shouts, "Lucien, it's time!"

"I'm going," says Lucien.

Lucien hesitates. He walks to and fro, looks at the city, then says to the boy, "Go home now."

The boy—all his little face is clenched in the attempt to grasp something of what's happening between the man and the stranger. But he does as he's told. He goes home. He goes and gets the stroller and then returns to the shack where his mother was a moment ago. The man waits for him to be gone before he goes himself.

The stranger hasn't moved.

He's still sitting, head bowed toward the ground, hands clasped, his arms resting on his knees.

He's the only one on the road now. His alone the road, the wilderness.

It's when he looks at him from a distance, through the window of the shack, that it occurs to the little boy that perhaps the stranger is dead, of a death that's miraculous, without anything seeming to have happened, without the semblance of death.

AURELIA PARIS

This is invented. A passion for the little Jewish girl who was abandoned.

I was always tempted to transpose "Aurélia Paris" for the stage. I did it for Gérard Desarthe. He gave a marvelous reading of it for two weeks in the Petite Salle of the Théâtre du Rond-Point in Paris in January 1984.

Today, beyond the windows, there's a forest, and the wind has started to blow. The roses were in that other, northern country. The little girl doesn't know about them. She never saw the roses, now dead, nor the fields, nor the sea.

The little girl is at the window in the tower, she's drawn the black curtains a little way apart and is looking out at the forest. It has stopped raining. It's almost night, but through the windowpane the sky is still blue. The tower is square, very tall, and made of black concrete. The little girl is on the top floor, she can see other towers here and there, also black. She has never been down into the forest.

The little girl goes away from the window and starts to sing a foreign song in a language she doesn't understand. You can still see quite well in the room. She looks at herself in the glass. She sees black hair and eyes that are bright. They are very dark blue. The little girl doesn't know that. Nor does she know she has always known the song. She can't remember having learned it.

Someone is crying. It's the lady who looks after her, feeds her and keeps her clean. The apartment is large and almost empty; almost everything has been sold. The lady's in the hall, sitting on a chair with a revolver beside her. The little girl has always known her like that, waiting for the German police. Night and day, the little girl doesn't know for how many years, the lady has been waiting. What the little girl does know is that as soon as the lady hears the word *polizei* outside the door she'll open it and kill everyone, first the others and then the two of them.

The little girl goes over and shuts the black, lined curtains, then goes over to her bed and switches on the little lamp on her desk. Under the lamp is the cat. The light disturbs it. Scattered around it are the papers telling about the latest operations of the army of the Reich, out of which the lady has taught the little girl to write. Stretched out stiffly beside the cat is a dead, dust-colored butterfly.

The little girl sits on the bed opposite the cat. The cat yawns, stretches, then sits down itself opposite her. Their eyes are on the same level. They look at each other. And now the little girl sings the Jewish song to the cat. The cat lies down on the table and the little girl strokes it, listens to it. Then she picks up the dead butterfly, shows it to the cat, looks at it and makes a funny face, then sings the Jewish song again. Then the cat's eyes and the eyes of the little girl look into each other again.

Suddenly, from far away in the sky, it arrives. The war. The noise. From the hall the lady calls out to her to draw the curtains, not to forget. The layers of steel start to pass over the forest. The lady calls out, "Talk to me."

"Still another six minutes," says the little girl. "Shut your eyes."

The roof of noise gets nearer, the cargo of death, the smooth bellies full of bombs, ready to open.

"They're here. Shut your eyes."

The little girl looks at her thin little hands on the cat. They're trembling like the walls, the window-panes, the air, the towers, the trees in the forest. The lady calls out, "Come here."

They're still going over. They take a little while longer than the little girl said they would. When the noise is at its height, suddenly there comes the other noise. The sharp shafts of the antiaircraft guns.

Nothing falls from the sky, nothing drops, nothing explodes. The solid mass of the squadron skims on unharmed across the sky.

"Where are they going?" cries the lady.

"Berlin," says the little girl.

"Come here."

The little girl crosses the dark room. Here's the lady. Here it's light. Here there's no window, nothing at all opening on the outside, it's the end of the hall, the front door, the place they'll come to. A light bulb hung up on the wall lights up the war. The lady is there to watch over the child's life. She has laid her knitting down in her lap. You can't hear anything now except the sound of guns taking over from one another in the distance. The little girl sits at the lady's feet and says, "The cat's killed a butterfly."

The lady and the little girl stay for a long while with their arms around one another, one weeping, the other cheerfully silent, as they do every evening. The lady says, "I've been crying again. Every day I weep for the amazing mistake that is life."

They laugh. The lady strokes the silky skeins, the black curls. The noise gets farther away. The little girl says, "They've crossed the Rhine."

There's no sound left but the gusts of wind in the forest. The lady has forgotten: "Where are they going?"

"Berlin," says the child.

"Oh yes, that's right."

They laugh. The lady asks, "What's going to become of us?"

"We're going to die," says the child. "You're going to kill us."

"Yes," says the lady. She stops laughing. "You're cold." She touches her arm.

The little girl doesn't answer. She laughs. She says, "I call the cat Aranacha."

"Aranachacha," repeats the lady.

The little girl laughs heartily. The lady laughs with her, then shuts her eyes and touches the little body.

"You're thin," says the lady. "Your little bones are almost sticking out."

The little girl laughs at everything the lady says. Often, in the evening, the little girl laughs at anything.

And now they're starting to sing the Jewish song. Then the lady tells her, "Apart from the little rectangle of white cotton sewn inside your dress, we don't know anything about you. It had the letters 'A.S.' on it and a date of birth. You're seven years old."

The little girl listens to the silence. She says, "They're over Berlin." She waits. "That's it."

She shoves the lady away, hits her, then gets up and

goes away. Goes through the corridors, doesn't knock into anything. The lady hears her singing.

The antiaircraft guns again, against the steel of the blue hulls. The little girl calls out to the lady. "Mission accomplished," she says. "They're coming back."

The noise gets louder—long, regular, a continuous wave. Not so heavy as on the way out.

"Not one's been hit," says the little girl.

"How many dead?" calls the lady.

"Fifty thousand," says the little girl.

The lady claps her hands.

"Lovely," says the lady.

"They're past the forest," says the little girl. "They're getting near the sea."

"Lovely. Lovely," says the lady.

"Listen," calls the little girl. "They're going to fly over the sea."

They wait.

"There," says the little girl. "They've flown over the sea."

The lady's talking to herself. She says all the children will be killed. The little girl laughs. She says to the cat, "She's crying. That's to make me go to her. She's frightened."

The little girl looks at herself in the glass and talks to herself. "I'm a Jewess," she says. "A Jew."

The little girl goes closer to the glass and looks at herself. "My mother kept a shop in the rue des Rosiers in Paris."

She points toward the hall: "She told me."

The little girl is speaking to the cat.

"Sometimes I want to die," says the little girl. She

adds, "I think my father was a traveler. He came from Syria."

In the distance, in the space outside, the drone begins again. The little girl calls out, "They're back again."

The lady has heard the second cargo of death. They wait.

"Where is it this time?"

The little girl shuts her eyes to hear better. "Düsseldorf," she says.

The little girl has hidden her face in her hands, she's frightened. In the distance the lady in the hall recites the names of the towns in the Palatinate and asks God to slaughter the German people.

"I'm frightened," says the little girl.

The lady hasn't heard.

The cat has gone, it's out in the corridors where there are no lights and the noise is not so loud.

"I'm frightened," says the little girl again.

"Are there many of them?" asks the lady.

"A thousand," says the little girl. "They're here."

Yes, they've reached the forest. They fly over. The electricity goes off.

"I wish they'd come down," cries the little girl. "I wish it would be over."

The lady calls out to the little girl to be quiet, it's shameful to talk like that.

The lady prays, recites in a high, mad voice a prayer she learned as a child. And then suddenly the child cries out in the dark, "The forest."

Suddenly the end of the world, a great scraping that ends in a crash. Din, uproar, and then fire, light.

Above, the squadron flies on.

The plane that's been shot down is left behind.

The little girl lifts a corner of the curtain and looks out at the fire. It's not far from the tower.

The little girl tries to make out the shape of the English airman. The lady shrieks out in the dark, "Come here, come here to me."

The little girl goes.

"It's an English plane. It came down just a little way away," says the little girl.

She says the forest is on fire just down there, a little way away from the tower. She says it's deserted except for the fire.

The little girl would like to go and see the plane that's come down. The lady says she doesn't want to see such a thing. The little girl insists. She says the pilot is dead, no, do come, it's only a fire.

The lady weeps, says it's useless.

"If I'd known . . . Well, don't let's talk about it, especially as I've nothing against the little girl herself . . . Only I'd have preferred it to be Jewish people who looked after her, and someone younger than I am . . . But what could I do? . . . Both of them taken away during the night, on a train made up of thirteen boxcars bound who knows where? And how could they ever prove she was their child now? But they might come back and say she is. Why not? . . . She's growing too fast; they say it's the lack of food . . . Seven years old according to the little white label in her sweater . . ."

The little girl listens to the lady. Sometimes she bursts out laughing and the lady wakes up. She asks what's the matter, who spoke, and where they went.

"Mannheim," says the little girl. "Or Frankfurt, or

Munich, or Leipzig, or Berlin"—she pauses—"or Nij-megen."

The lady says she loves the little girl, very much. Then she is silent. Then she says again she loves her, and how much. The little girl shakes her gently. She says, "So she ran upstairs, carrying a little girl?"

"That's right."

"Who?"

"Your mother," says the lady.

" 'Take the baby—I've got an urgent errand to do,' " says the little girl.

"That's right. 'I've got an urgent errand to do. I'll be back in ten minutes.' "

"There was a noise on the stairs?"

"Yes. The German police."

"And then nothing."

"No."

"Never, ever?"

"Never."

The little girl puts her head on the lady's knees so the lady can stroke her hair.

The lady strokes the little girl's hair hard, just as she likes her to, and talks to her about her own, the little girl's life. Then her hand stops. She asks, "So, where are these people now?"

"Liège," says the little girl. "They're going home."

The little girl asks the lady, "Who was the one that died?"

The lady tells a story about an English airman.

The little girl hugs the lady. The lady protests.

"Kiss me, kiss me," says the little girl.

The lady makes an effort and strokes the little girl's

hair, then sleep gets the better of her. One after another the sirens in the city sound the all clear.

"Tell me his name," says the little girl.

"Whose?" says the lady.

"Anyone you like."

"Steiner," says the lady. "That was what the police were shouting."

The cat. It comes back from another room.

"They're back," says the little girl. "They're going to fly over the sea."

The little girl starts to stroke the cat, at first absent-mindedly and then harder and harder. She says, "He ate a fly, too."

The lady listens. She says, "I can't hear them coming back."

"They went the northern route," says the little girl.

Already, at the windows, it's light. The light shines into the corridor of war.

The cat lies on its back, purring with passionate desire for Aurélia. Aurélia lies down beside it. She says, "My mother's name was Steiner."

Aurélia puts her head on the cat's belly. The cat's belly is warm, it holds the cat's purring, a vast buried continent.

"Steiner, Aurélia. Like me."

Still this room I write to you from. Today, beyond the windows, there was the forest, and the wind had started to blow.

The roses have died in that other, northern country, one rose after another, carried off by winter.

It's dark. I can't see the words I've written any more. I can't see anything except my motionless hand which has stopped writing to you. But through the window-pane the sky is still blue. The blue of Aurélia's eyes would have been darker, you know, especially in the evening, when it had lost its color and become clear, unfathomable darkness.

My name is Aurélia Steiner.

I live in Paris. My parents are teachers there.

I'm eighteen.

I write.

About the Author

One of the most important literary figures in France, Marguerite Duras is best known in the United States for her brilliant filmscript *Hiroshima, Mon Amour* and her novel *The Lover*. She is the author of many novels and screenplays. Marguerite Duras was born in Indochina in 1914 and lives in Paris.